Women Icons
of the West

〜〜

JULIE DANNEBERG

Women Icons
of the West

FIVE WOMEN WHO FORGED
THE AMERICAN FRONTIER

FULCRUM PUBLISHING
GOLDEN, COLORADO

Library of Congress Cataloging-in-Publication Data

Danneberg, Julie, 1958-
 Women icons of the West : five women who forged the American frontier
/ Julie Danneberg.
     p. cm. -- (Notable Western women)
 Includes bibliographical references and index.
 ISBN 978-1-55591-745-6 (pbk.)
1. Women pioneers--West (U.S.)--Biography. 2. Women--West
(U.S.)--Biography. 3. Frontier and pioneer life--West (U.S.) 4. West
(U.S.)--Biography. I. Title.
 F596.D274 2010
 920.720978--dc22

                              2009049797

Special thanks to the historical artifact collections of Marjorie Maher, Susan Zernial, Julie Maher, and Kathy Kirchhoff

Printed in Canada
0 9 8 7 6 5 4 3 2 1

Design by Margaret McCullough

Fulcrum Publishing
4690 Table Mountain Drive, Suite 100
Golden, Colorado 80403
800-992-2908 • 303-277-1623
www.fulcrumbooks.com

Contents

﹏

Introduction

❦❦

WOMEN ICONS OF THE WEST is a colorful collection of biographies of five women who braved the western frontier. At first glance, each woman seems vastly different: Isabella Bird, a refined Englishwoman venturing into untamed wilderness; Clara Brown, a newly freed slave just tasting her freedom; Margaret Brown, a miner's wife turned millionaire/society woman; Nellie Cashman, a caregiving wanderer trying her hand at prospecting; and Sarah Winnemucca, a Native American fighting against the loss of her culture. However, despite their outward differences, these women have much in common and much to teach us about hardships and perseverance.

But there is another reason to study these women. To truly understand history, you should be familiar with the people who lived and worked during each time period. These women bring a variety of western experiences to our awareness. To understand the West, we need to hear the voices of all its citizens—men and women, rich and poor, all cultures, ages, and religions. *Women Icons of the West* allows these women's voices to be heard, along with the thoughts of the people who knew them.

While you are getting acquainted with these amazing women, it is important to realize that this book is a work of creative nonfiction. Although the facts, places, dates, and events are all accurate, the means used to capture them is fictional narrative. Isabella Bird's innkeeper in Greeley, Colorado, never told her version of Isabella's visit, but after reading the research, it is easy to imagine what she might have said. Clara Brown's fellow wagon-train

OPPOSITE: *Georgetown, Colorado, circa 1901, by William Henry Jackson. Photo courtesy of the Library of Congress.*

travelers never spoke about their shared journey, but knowing the prejudices and facts of the time, one can see that these imagined conversations convey common feelings held by many.

This book offers a deeper understanding of each woman by showing her life in relationship to the world around her. Simply put, a biography that switches between the first and third person allows us to see the West through the eyes of each woman and to see each woman through the eyes of the West. The American West in the late 1800s was a challenging, exhilarating, and often scary place. I hope you enjoy meeting some of the women who lived there at such an exciting time.

Isabella Bird

(1831–1904)

C OULD YOU RIDE A HORSE FOR NINE HOURS, through deep snow and temperatures so cold that your boots freeze to the stirrups? Would you travel alone in the winter, through the Colorado Rocky Mountains, without even a map to show you the way? Could you sleep in an unheated log cabin with cracks so wide that the snow drifts in and covers you while you sleep? Isabella Bird did all these things and more. And she did them more than 120 years ago.

Born in Yorkshire, England, in 1831, Isabella was a frail and sickly child. She had a bad back that kept her in bed much of the time. At seventeen, she had an operation to remove a tumor from her spine, but even that didn't seem to improve her health. As a last resort, the doctor prescribed a relaxing trip. The excited twenty-three-year-old embarked on her first trip abroad, traveling to Canada and the United States. Although conditions were difficult and her schedule hectic, Isabella never felt better. She positively blossomed under the "strain" of travel.

The letters Isabella wrote home described all of her adventures. When she returned, her father encouraged her to make them into a book. *The Englishwoman in America*, published in 1856, was a big success.

Twenty years later, Isabella was on the last leg of another trip that included Australia, New Zealand, Hawaii, and San Francisco. Having heard about the glorious, untamed beauty of the Rocky Mountains, she decided she wanted to experience the Wild West firsthand. This is the story of her three month-trip to the Colorado Territory in 1873.

OPPOSITE: *Isabella Bird, looking very much the Victorian lady at seventy years old. Photo courtesy of the Denver Public Library Western History Collection.*

ISABELLA: SEPTEMBER 9, 1873

The sight out of the train window today contrasted sharply with the sights, sounds, and smells inside the train. Outside, the mountains heaved themselves up from the plains into five distinct zigzag ranges. Blue rock against blue sky, their grandeur left me breathless. Unfortunately, this truly grand sight was viewed from inside a railroad car where I was unhappily surrounded by chewing, spitting Yankees. I must say I am thoroughly repulsed by this western custom of chewing tobacco. The stench is abominable. I can hardly approve of such a distasteful habit!

WANTED: WOMEN

Gold was first discovered in Colorado in the summer of 1858. By the next year, thousands of adventurers and goldseekers had flooded the territory. Most of these newcomers were men. In the 1860 census, Colorado's population consisted of 33,000 men and 1,600 women—about one woman for every twenty men. By 1870, the figures had changed dramatically, with 25,000 men and 15,000 women. This figure is misleading, however, because in the small mountain mining camps and the railroad towns dotting the prairie, the vast majority of citizens still remained men.

FEMALE INNKEEPER: GREELEY, SEPTEMBER 9, 1873

I met Isabella Bird when she bustled into my boardinghouse looking for a place to stay. Speaking with a crisp English accent, she asked for a room.

"Yes, there is a bed available," I answered briefly. I didn't have time for pleasantries, although I longed for female company. When you run a boardinghouse, pleasure is in short supply and work isn't. I needed to get dinner on the table for twenty hungry men. Miss Bird, for all her fancy clothes, jumped in and helped, although I could tell that she was a stranger to work. I don't suppose an English lady fills her day with cooking, washing, or sweeping. Oh, well. She'll find things are different here.

ISABELLA: SEPTEMBER 9, 1873

My room was not a room at all but a makeshift, stuffy space, fashioned by hanging canvas walls from the ceiling. I had difficulty falling asleep as I heard every whisper, cough, and snore. Then I awoke in the middle of the night itching and scratching from head to toe. Striking a match, I gasped to find myself and my bed crawling with swarms of bugs.

After such an unsettling night, I eagerly accepted a wagon ride into the mountains when the chance presented itself.

Mrs. Chalmers: Big Thompson Canyon, September 12, 1873

'Afore we came here from back East, Mr. Chalmers was sick, laid low by tuberculosis. We heard that the mountain air in Colorado helped people like him get better. We came and sure 'nuf, Mr. Chalmers got well.

When that woman first showed up here, I figured that she was lookin' for the cure, too. But no, she said she came to see the mountains. Can you imagine such foolishness? A grown woman cavortin' around the countryside all alone. Humph! She asked for a room. And though I saw no good in this citified woman's silly travels, I said she could stay for five dollars a week. "As long as you make yourself agreeable," I told her.

ISABELLA

Agreeable? My word! I almost left when that pinched, uneducated woman told me that I had to make myself agreeable in this, the most disagreeable of places. The Chalmerses had a squatter's claim of 160 acres of land and lived here many years under the most uncivilized of conditions. Their family of seven squeezed into a falling-down, two-room log cabin with no beds, no furniture to speak of, and not even a fastening on the door. When I saw this and saw my ride rattle away, faced with the Chalmerses unfriendliness, I just sat down and knitted. After a while, I regained my composure enough to eat the supper they placed silently beside me: dried beef and milk.

As soon as darkness fell, the family dragged their straw mattresses and blankets outside to sleep under the stars. I preferred inside by the fire. I often heard tiny animals scurrying across the floor and once awoke to find myself looking into the eyes of a snake. The next morning, in an effort to make myself "agreeable," I offered to do the dishes.

MRS. CHALMERS

When that woman asked to wash the dishes, I done shook my head, disbelievin'. I said, "I'm guessin' you'll make more work than you'll do. I see those hands of yours, all smooth and white. Never done a stitch of work, I bet. No, thank you. I'll do the dishes myself."

A CREATIVE SOLUTION

Riding through the Rocky Mountains, Isabella spent many hours at a time in the saddle. But she had a problem. Riding sidesaddle, as the etiquette of the time required, was uncomfortable and hurt her back. To solve this problem, Isabella wore what she called her "Hawaiian riding dress." Underneath a split skirt reaching to the feet were bloomers that gathered at the ankle. When sitting on a horse, the bloomers allowed her to ride astride. When she was standing, the skirt fell very properly and looked like a regular skirt. Very smart! Isabella could look like a lady and ride like a man.

Isabella: Longmont, End of September, 1873

I stayed with the Chalmerses for over a week and never reached my goal of getting farther into the mountains. Defeated, I returned to a hotel on the prairie, in Longmont.

Platt Rogers: End of September, 1873

My friend Sylvester Downer and I had long looked forward to our mountain holiday. We were spending the night in Longmont before taking on the last leg of our journey, the long hard ride into Estes Park. The proprietor of our hotel asked us to take along a female hotel guest. Said he'd consider it a personal favor. Naturally, we said yes, although inwardly I feared the presence of a woman might prove a hindrance. "Oh well, maybe she'll be young and beautiful," we comforted ourselves. My hopes were dashed the next morning when I first saw Miss Bird. She wore strange-looking bloomers, rode like a man, and was neither young nor beautiful.

We began our ride, and I was relieved to find that Miss Bird did not slow our progress.

A sketch of the Estes Park valley, where Isabella stayed in a guest cabin belonging to Griff Evans. Image courtesy of the Denver Public Library Western History Collection.

MOUNTAIN MAN

Mountain Jim had a squatter's claim to land in Estes Park. He roamed the land trapping beaver and other animals, selling the meat and skins to men in Denver. He was well known throughout the West as a desperado. In fact, Isabella was warned, "When he's sober, Jim's a perfect gentleman; but when he's had liquor, he's the most awful ruffian in Colorado."

MOUNTAIN JIM: NEAR ESTES PARK, END OF SEPTEMBER, 1873

I met the gracious and lovely Miss Isabella Bird when she first passed my home on her way to Estes Park.

My proper name is James Nugent, but I am known as Mountain Jim, partly because of my skills as a hunter and trapper and partly because of my untamed behavior. My home is at the edge of Estes Park, a wide and wild river valley sitting in the shadow of tall granite mountains. The hunting here is plentiful and the people are not. That is why I like it.

ISABELLA

On the approach to Estes Park, we passed a rustic cabin that looked more like the den of a wild beast than the home of a human. Furs of lynx, bear, and other animals dried on the roof, and a wisp of smoke puffed leisurely out of the chimney. A deer carcass hung at one end of the cabin. A large collie growled a greeting. Out came a rough mountain man dressed in a buckskin suit, with a knife tucked in his belt and a revolver sticking out of his breast pocket. His hair, a messy tangle of long blond curls, partially hid the scars that rippled half his face. I found out later the scars came from a fight with a bear.

Mr. Nugent kicked the dog angrily and then raised his hat to me. "Is there anything I can do for you?" he asked very politely, with the hint of a foreign accent.

"Something to drink, if you please," I replied.

He bowed as he handed me water in a battered tin cup.

Before we rode on, he asked if he could call on me tomorrow. Most disconcerting. I could see that Mr. Nugent looked like the most unsavory of characters, and yet his gentle voice and cultured speech told me there was more to this man.

Griffith Evans:
End of September, 1873
Good day to you, my friend. I am Griffith Evans. My partner and I run this cattle ranch. I'm a Welshman and like Miss Bird, I too am far from my native land. Ah, but I like it here. The great stretch of wild land and the open expanse of blue sky sometimes remind me of home, don'tcha know.

Miss Bird rambled into the ranch late one afternoon asking for a place to stay. "All are welcome," I said, shakin' her hand and givin' her my best smile. For eight dollars a week, she received room and board and the unlimited use of a horse— when she could catch one, that is.

Isabella: Longs Peak,
Early October, 1873
Longs Peak was absolutely beautiful. I've seen mountains all over Europe and none can compare. That scraggly old mountain stood guard over the whole valley. After a few days in its shadow, I wanted to become better acquainted with the mountain. Mr. Evans warned me that only twice before had a woman made it to the summit. Mr. Nugent reminded me that in October, storms hit unexpected. *Pish posh*, I thought to myself. *I will do it*. So I badgered and begged

IS IT LOVE?

In the years since *A Lady's Life in the Rocky Mountains* was published, there has been much speculation about whether there actually was a romance between Isabella and Mountain Jim. It is hard to imagine a more unlikely match. When writing home to her sister Henrietta, Isabella once described Jim as "a man any woman could love but no sane woman would marry." That about says it all.

When he spoke to her on their first meeting, Isabella said, "I forgot both his reputation and appearance for his manner was that of a chivalrous gentleman, his accent refined, and his language easy and elegant."

PRESERVED FOREVER

The beautiful untamed wilderness that Isabella fell in love with still exists more than a hundred years later. Part of the area where Isabella roamed has been made into Rocky Mountain National Park. This 265,000-acre area contains towering peaks, rolling meadows, and dense forests. More than seventy-five peaks stand 12,000 feet or more above sea level. Longs Peak, at 14,255 feet, is the highest point in the park.

IF THE SHOE FITS

Because she had no shoes suitable for climbing a mountain, Isabella started out on her hike wearing Mr. Evans's boots. The boots were too big and made climbing very awkward. "Fortunately, before the real difficulty of the ascent began, we found, under a rock, a pair of small overshoes." These boots probably belonged to Anna Dickinson, who had made the climb earlier that year.

PASS THE MEAT AND POTATOES, PLEASE

If you don't like vegetables, then living the frontier life might have been the life for you. Obviously, no fresh fruits or vegetables grew in the mountains in the winter. Canned food was available in stores, but to people like Griffith Evans, who live far away from stores, eating canned food was a luxury not available.

until finally, in the face of my stubbornness, Mr. Nugent agreed to take me.

Accompanied by my two riding companions, Mr. Rogers and Mr. Downer, Mr. Nugent and I left early in the morning. Behind my saddle I carried three pairs of camping blankets, a quilt, and enough steak, bread, and tea to last me three days.

The first day we rode our horses to tree line, making camp about three thousand feet below the summit. We cooked our steaks over a roaring fire and ate them without forks or plates, juices dripping through our fingers.

Pine boughs covered with a blanket made a lumpy but fragrant bed. That night, the wind, rumbling down from Longs Peak, kept me awake.

Dawn came with air so cold it burned my lungs when I breathed. We began our climb. I looked up to see sheer rock towering above me. Mr. Nugent tied me to a rope and then tied the rope to himself. In this manner, hour after endless hour, we inched our way up the steep, unyielding slopes, sliding on loose stone and ice, looking down sheer, unforgiving cliffs.

PLATT ROGERS

This time Miss Bird did slow down our progress. Sylvester and I went on ahead. Mountain Jim dragged Miss Bird up that mountain, shoving and lifting her like a bale of hay. I have to give her credit, though—she didn't complain, even though she looked close to dead with effort by the time she made it to the summit.

ISABELLA

I made it to the summit—barely. And only thanks to Mr. Nugent. The view from the top was worth all the pain achieving it. Before me lay Colorado. I felt humbled by the thought that I stood where few had stood before.

As we turned to retrace our steps, I fought back tears of fatigue. We struggled and scrambled and slid back down the mountain. When we made it back to camp after dark, I rolled myself up in a blanket and went promptly to sleep.

A present-day view of Longs Peak. Image courtesy of Shutterstock.

DEAR SIS

Isabella figured out an ingenious way to write her books. On a regular basis, she wrote letters home to her sister, Henrietta. In spidery, difficult-to-read penmanship she wrote detailed explanations of everything she did and saw. She also made sketches, which were translated into pictures for the book by artist Charles Whymper.

HOW DID THE STORY END?

About six months after Isabella last saw Mountain Jim, she received the horrible news that he was dead. After a quarrel, Griffith Evans shot Jim as he rode past Evans's cabin. Mountain Jim was severely wounded and eventually died from his injuries.

Isabella: Mid-October, 1873

At the Evans' ranch my days followed a pleasing rhythm. At seven o'clock, I joined the Evans family. We breakfasted on beef, potatoes, tea, new bread, and butter, washing it all down with fresh milk. On the way back to my cabin, I drew icy water from the lake to wash my clothes. Then I read and wrote letters to my sister, Henrietta, until dinner at noon.

Mr. Nugent visited almost every afternoon. He recited poetry as we explored the park or rode to check on his traps.

Famished by six o'clock tea, I feasted on the same food as at breakfast, of which there was never a shortage, although it seemed Mrs. Evans was always up to her elbows in bread dough. The meat was carved, piece by piece, from a steer that hung in the corner of the kitchen.

Mr. Evans

By jove, I did like Miss Bird! Always ready to help, she was. Early one morning I pounded on her cabin door. "We need an extra hand," I said. "Are you game?" Miss Bird said yes without a moment's hesitation. I never used a woman on one of my cattle roundups, but she lived up to the challenge just fine. What a horsewoman! Tearing after loose cattle, weaving in and out of trees at breakneck speed, ducking and dodging broken branches, you'd think she'd done it all her life.

LAVA BEDS, LONG'S PEAK.

An illustration from A Lady's Life in the Rocky Mountains. *Courtesty of the Library of Congress.*

ISABELLA

That night a blizzard struck. I huddled in bed shivering under six blankets as the wind screeched and whistled through every nook and cranny of my cabin. Every once in a while, above the steady roar, I heard the thundering explosions of breaking branches. The next morning I awoke to find the sheet frozen to my lips and my bed thickly covered with snow. The wind had driven snow through the cracks of my cabin wall.

MR. EVANS

The blizzard lasted for more than three days, telling me it was time to pack up my family and get us down to Denver for the winter. I offered Miss Bird six dollars a week to stay on to feed and water the livestock. She just laughed and said, "No, thank you."

When the road was cleared of drifts, Miss Bird saddled up and rode for Denver, too. I loaned her a horse named Birdie.

HENRIETTA BIRD: ENGLAND, MID-OCTOBER, 1873

Honestly, sometimes I almost believed it was a different woman writing me those letters of her adventures in the West. Surely it could not be my own sister, Isabella, riding around like a wild savage, forgetting all propriety. I lived in constant fear for her safety.

ISABELLA: DENVER, COLORADO, MID-OCTOBER, 1873

It took me two days to ride to Denver. Crossing the brown, snow-covered plains, the intense cold and biting wind cut right through to the bone. I passed herds of grazing cattle and horses and saw many white-topped prairie schooners lumbering along, sometimes alone, sometimes in trains.

One such group invited me to join them for the midday meal. They provided the hominy, and I the tea. They left Illinois three months ago with all of their worldly possessions crammed into their wagon. One of their children died en route. They seemed tired, weak, and disheartened.

After I left them, I passed a herd of two thousand lean Texas cattle, driven by three men on horseback and followed by two wagons filled with women and children.

I raced a snowstorm into Denver. As I went to sleep in a warm bed, my thoughts returned to the schooner family camping out in the midst of this cold.

WILLIAM BYERS, EDITOR OF THE *Rocky Mountain News*: DENVER, COLORADO, LATE OCTOBER, 1873

Miss Isabella Bird came into my office and introduced herself. To tell the truth, I already knew about the Englishwoman who climbed Longs Peak. After all, it is my business to know what's going on around the territory. I must admit, though, to a bit of surprise when I first met her. I'm not sure what I expected, but this short, rather matronly woman of middle age certainly wasn't it.

I took her to meet Governor Hunt and together the three of us mapped out a route for her to see more of Colorado.

A sketch of Isabella looking quite jaunty in her Hawaiian riding outfit. Image courtesy of the Denver Public Library Western History Collection.

I admire Miss Bird's courage. There aren't many ladies who would ride out into the Colorado Territory alone.

ISABELLA: LATE OCTOBER, 1873

Denver is a hustling, bustling city of the frontier. It boasts wide streets, electric street lamps, wooden sidewalks, and even a library. That is, in addition to the usual brothels and saloons. I saw only five women all day long but encountered many men, from every walk of life, sporting every style of dress: hunters and trappers in buckskin clothes, men in great blue cloaks left over from the war, horsemen in fur coats, caps, and hairy buffalo hide boots, rich English sporting tourists, and suited businessmen.

COLORFUL CHARACTERS

Throughout her travels, Isabella met many colorful characters. On the long ride between Colorado Springs and Denver, she was joined by an unknown horseman. Describing him, she said, "He wore a big slouch hat, from under which a number of fair curls hung nearly to his waist. He was dressed in a hunter's buckskin suit ornamented with beads, and wore a pair of exceptionally big brass spurs. What was unusual was the number of weapons he carried. Besides a rifle laid across his saddle and a pair of pistols in the holsters, he carried two revolvers and a knife in his belt and a carbine slung behind him. I found him what is termed good company."

The stranger turned out to be Comanche Bill, one of the most notorious desperadoes of the Rocky Mountains!

There were also hundreds of Indians on their small ponies, wearing beaded buckskin and red blankets.

Being in the midst of such colorful liveliness left me dazed and tired. My ears have grown accustomed to the quiet of nature and the peace of the mountains. I eagerly left the city behind, riding sidesaddle until I reached the plains.

DENVER RESIDENT: LATE OCTOBER, 1873

I read about Miss Isabella Bird, the traveling Englishwoman, in the newspaper today. A woman's place is in the home, not climbing mountains and dashing around on horseback. It isn't respectable, and I suspect she'll face her comeuppance soon enough.

ISABELLA: LATE OCTOBER, 1873

Sometimes the snow was so deep, I got off and walked, breaking the trail for Birdie. I rode for hours without seeing a soul. The only sounds were Birdie's warm, even breathing, the crunch of snow beneath our feet, the creak of my saddle, and the hushed whisper of wind through the trees.

It is the custom here for settlers to take in travelers, giving them room and board for a fee. This arrangement is a sensible one, but I learned to be prepared for any accommodations. One night I stayed in a house so cold, and with blankets so thin, that in the middle of the night I pulled the rag rug right up off the floor and used it as another blanket! The next night I stayed at the lovely home of Mr. Perry, a millionaire cattle rancher.

A VICTORIAN LADY

To understand Isabella's background is to more fully appreciate her accomplishments. Middle- and upper-class women were expected to marry and have a family. These women considered the everyday work of running the household beneath them. Their day was spent paying visits, sewing, and overseeing the servants. It was the servants who cooked, cleaned, and took care of the children.

Miss Perry, Daughter of Mr. Perry

I understand the call, the excitement of travel, but when I take a trip, it won't be to go deeper into the wilderness, it will be toward civilization and culture. When I met her, I admired Miss Bird's courage, but I questioned her ability to survive the trip. Such a proper English lady, what could she possibly know about a Rocky Mountain winter? Before she left the house I gave her a pair of Father's socks to put over her boots, explaining that they might keep her feet from slipping if she had to walk on the ice or snow. As she rode away into the swirling snow and icy winter winds, I felt sorry for her. Obviously she had no idea what she was in for.

Isabella: Colorado City, End of October, 1873

Five days and 150 snow-covered miles later, I reached a tiny cluster of houses called Colorado City. I stopped, put on a long skirt, made myself presentable, and rode a few more miles west into Colorado Springs.

CAN I BORROW YOUR HORSE?

After Isabella settled into her hotel in Georgetown, she asked if anyone would loan her a horse to ride up to Green Lake. "The Landlord said he thought not; the snow was very deep, and no one had been up for five weeks, but for my satisfaction he would send to a stable and inquire. The amusing answer came back, If it's the English lady traveling in the mountains she can have a horse, but not any one else."

Landlady: Colorado Springs, End of October, 1873

Miss Bird spent a night in my boardinghouse. On the night of her stay, some poor man lay dying from consumption in one of the bedrooms while the rest of my guests visited and played cards in the parlor.

Isabella: Denver, Colorado, End of October, 1873

Ice, snow, blue skies, and blizzards. That describes my return trip to Denver. I must admit, though, that I got quite good at finding and staying to a trail. I received such strange directions: "Follow some wheel marks till you get to some timber and keep to the north till you come to a creek." As you might imagine, I was grateful every night to find a place to stay.

GEORGETOWN MINER: MID-NOVEMBER, 1873

I met Miss Bird at the hotel in Georgetown where we both were guests. She came in long after dark, her cheeks a rosy red and the air around her crackling with excitement. I gladly listened while she told me of her adventure. After arriving in Georgetown, she hired a horse and traveled farther up the mountain to Green Lake. She reached her destination just as the sun sank majestically behind the mountain. She told me that she didn't know which was more breathtaking, the sunset or the dangerous ride back down the dark, narrow, icy trail!

ISABELLA: BOULDER, COLORADO, MID-NOVEMBER, 1873

I returned to Golden City the same way I came, through Clear Creek Canyon, on the narrow-gauge train. I saw evidence of mining everywhere. The walls of the canyon were ugly and bare, all the trees having been cut to build the mines. A constant roar rumbled up from the blasting, milling, and smelting that goes on day and night.

In Golden, I retrieved Birdie from the town stable and set out for Boulder, but soon lost my way on the plains. The sun set, the stars came out, the cold descended, and I have never felt so alone—one tiny speck on the endless prairie. Hour after hour, Birdie and I plodded on, ears perked and eyes peeled.

Finally, about midnight, I stumbled upon a house. The gift of human companionship had never seemed more dear. The next day I reached Boulder.

With winter setting in fast and hard, I knew it was time to return home. But I couldn't go without a final glimpse of Estes Park. As I rode away the last time, I knew that the beauty and splendor of the magnificent Rocky Mountains would stay forever in my heart.

Isabella at her writing desk, where she turned her detailed letters into best-selling travel books.
Photo courtesy of the Colorado Historical Society.

∾ *Afterword* ∾

Isabella left Colorado on December 11, 1873. She never returned to the Rocky Mountains. She did continue to live a life of adventure, however, traveling all over the world to places like China, Tibet, and Persia. Many of the places she went had never been visited by a European woman before. Isabella also continued to write books about her adventures and became one of the best-known travel writers of her day. In fact, in 1892 she was honored as the first woman member of the exclusive Royal Geographic Society.

Isabella created a life that suited her, one of excitement, adventure, and challenge. This was unusual for a woman of her day, but then again, Isabella was truly a woman ahead of her time.

❧ *Bibliography* ❧

Barr, Pat. *A Curious Life for a Lady.* London: Macmillan/John Murray, 1970.

Bird, Isabella L. *A Lady's Life in the Rocky Mountains.* New ed. Norman: Univ. of Oklahoma Press, 1960.

Birkett, Dea. *Spinsters Abroad: Victorian Lady Explorers.* New York: Basil Blackwell, 1989.

Dunning, Harold M. *The Life of Rocky Mountain Jim (James Nugent).* Boulder, CO: Johnson Publishing, 1967.

Kaye, Evelyn. *Amazing Traveler: Isabella Bird.* Boulder, CO: Blue Penguin Publications, 1994.

Robertson, Janet. *The Magnificent Mountain Women: Adventures in the Colorado Rockies.* Lincoln: Univ. of Nebraska Press, 1990.

Stoddart, Anna M. *The Life of Isabella Bird (Mrs. Bishop).* London: John Murray, 1906.

Tinling, Marion. *Women into the Unknown: A Sourcebook on Women Explorers and Travelers.* New York: Greenwood Press, 1989.

Clara Brown

(1800–1885)

〰〰

C AN YOU IMAGINE THE UNFAIRNESS OF BEING BORN A SLAVE? The indignity of being treated like a possession instead of a human being? The grief of having your children taken from you to be sold at the auction block? This was the life Clara Brown was born into in 1800.

Clara had no formal education and, like many people of her time, both black and white, could neither read nor write. Yet, after she was freed, through hard work and a commonsense approach to business, she earned a great deal of money. Even then she continued to live a simple life, willingly spending all that she earned to help others. But the most amazing thing about Clara Brown wasn't her business success or her generosity, but that she didn't allow herself to grow angry or bitter. Her deep faith in God kept her full of hope in even the most dismal situations.

GOING, GOING, GONE

I n 1835, Clara watched as, one by one, her family was auctioned off to different owners. Her husband and son were sold to slave traders and probably sent downriver to work on a cotton plantation. This was the worst possible fate for a slave, since those who labored in the fields had the shortest life expectancy. Clara's daughters, Margaret and Eliza Jane, were sold to two different owners closer to home, but she had no way of communicating with them and soon lost touch.

OPPOSITE: *Seventy-year-old Clara Brown poses for the camera wearing a black dress and crocheted black cap. Photo courtesy of the Denver Public Library Western History Collection.*

DIFFICULT MEANS OF TRAVEL

In 1859 it was against the law for a black person to pay for a ticket on public transportation. A black person could only travel as a servant accompanying a white person. Passage on the wagon train at that time usually cost around $550. That was a lot of money in those days. Even if Clara could have paid for her ticket, she wouldn't have been allowed to.

COLONEL WADSWORTH: LEAVENWORTH, KANSAS, APRIL 1859

By gosh, I had a stroke of good luck when I met Clara Brown. She came looking for work, and I hired her right there on the spot. I was getting the wagon train organized and needed someone to cook for the single men. Clara needed a way west, so we worked out a deal.

Tall, lanky, and strong, Clara seemed to be in good health. I asked her why she'd want to travel west on a wagon train, being fifty-seven years of age. She told me her story, a real sad one, although not that unusual, I'm afraid. Seems she wanted to find her daughter Eliza Jane. They were separated twenty-four years ago, when Eliza Jane was eleven, sold as a slave. Clara thinks that her daughter's owner might have taken her west. Maybe. There sure are a whole lot of people headin' that way. Yep, I guess anything is possible.

WAGON-TRAIN TRAVELER 1

I'm glad that Clara came along when she did. I needed someone to cook my meals for me. I sure weren't plannin' on fixin' dinner for myself after I'd spent all day in the saddle or driving one of those hard-on-the-back wagons. And I especially weren't plannin' on getting up early to fix myself breakfast. That's woman's work and I don't do woman's work.

What with the long days, hot sun, and cold wind, life out on the prairie was miserable. I knew I'd be able to take it better on a full stomach.

CLARA

Lordy, how folks on that wagon train complained. They told me their feet hurt, they missed their home, and they were sick of breathin' in and coughin'

This oxen-powered wagon train rumbling over the prairie looks much like the one Clara took from Leavenworth, Kansas, to Denver, Colorado. Photo courtesy of the Denver Public Library Western History Collection.

up dust all day long. I heard it all. But you didn't hear me saying a single bad word. Lord almighty, no. I've known hard times before, and let me tell you that trip weren't nothin'. Sure, I worked hard, but I was a free woman. I just praise the Lord my skill carried me, even if it was sometimes a hard job for these two old feet of mine.

I thought, "Maybe I'll find my Eliza Jane," with all these folks headin' west. Lord knows I'd been lookin' for her everywhere, askin' everyone I met if they've seen her. I kept wondering to myself, how big is this here world that I can't find my own kin?

HAVE YOU SEEN MY DAUGHTER?

Clara's last owners valued her and treated her kindly. One way they showed their affection and high regard for her was by trying to help find her daughter Eliza Jane. They spent time and money writing letters to friends and neighbors inquiring where she might have been sold.

FREE AT LAST!

Clara gained her freedom in 1857. When she did, she was given her "freedom papers." She had to carry these papers wherever she went as proof that she was not a runaway slave. She also had one year to leave the state. If she didn't, her freedom would be revoked and she'd automatically become a slave again.

Wagon-Train Traveler 2

I'm glad that the wagon master hired Clara to come along. But that doesn't mean we should treat her any different than we treat all the slaves back home. She's lucky we let her come with us. She shouldn't've expected no special privileges on top of that. As far as I was concerned, she'd sleep on the ground and eat by herself after she served us. That was plenty good for her kind.

Wagon-Train Traveler 3

Hush, now. You might have had slaves where you came from, but this ain't the South. You best remember that and keep your pro-slavery feelings to yourself. The West is mainly anti-slavery. Sometime you can explain to me why you think one man has the right to own another. But not today—I got too much work to do. The fact is that Clara isn't even a slave. She is a free woman and she has the papers to prove it.

HOW I SPENT MY SPRING BREAK

Days on the wagon train followed a pattern. The day began at 4 AM, when the cooking fires were rekindled from the night before. Breakfast was made and eaten, and then the dishes were cleaned and put away. Everyone needed to be ready to start traveling by 7 AM. The wagon train stopped for a break around noon so the oxen could be watered and rested. The wagon train started back up again at 2:00 in the afternoon and traveled until around 5 or 6 PM.

Clara: May 1859

Lordy, I think that the boredom was the hardest part of the trip. Every day it was the same, walkin' mile after mile through the tall grass and dry dust. I felt mighty small with that big ocean of prairie stretchin' out as far as the

An illustration of buffalo and antelope on prairie, much like Clara would have seen. Photo courtesy of the Library of Congress.

eye could see. The weather rolled through with the clouds, cool in the mornin' but heatin' up like a cookstove by midday.

We ate mostly bacon and salt pork, morning, noon, and night. A person can get mighty tired of the same meal three times a day, no matter how good it is. So I said, "Glory be and praise the Lord," when I saw the buffalo herd. I knew a change in our diet was moving in right before our very eyes.

It was a hot day and the sun was beating down on the prairie. The smell of the buffalo reached our noses almost 'afore the sight of them reached our eyes. Hundreds of them stretched out, a dark brown blanket covering the rolling prairie hills. Captain Wadsworth sent some

LOAD 'EM UP

Obviously, the travelers couldn't stop at a grocery store to replenish their food supplies. Most of what they ate they had to carry with them. Bacon and salt pork were the staple meats. Each wagon also carried flour, sugar, coffee, rice, tea, dried apples, and water kegs. Other provisions might have included simple medications, vinegar, soap, matches, basic cooking utensils, and a field stove or sheet iron to cook on over a fire.

men out with rifles. When the shots sounded, I saw a few buffalo crumple down into dark woolly heaps, dead as can be. The rest took off, running away from us. Lord almighty, what a glorious sight! So many pounding hooves. Even at a distance I felt the earth shake.

Who'da thought a poor old woman like me would have so many adventures? I just wish my family could have shared that glorious day with me. But then, maybe Eliza Jane has seen equally wondrous sights. I know I won't rest easy until I find her. I can't enjoy anything full up without knowing whether she's okay.

CLARA: JUNE 1859

I don't mind telling you that the closer we got to Denver, the more nervous I got. I had my laundry tubs and equipment. I expected that Denver would provide me with plenty of work, with its muddy streets and dirty men. But Lordy, I was scared. Every time I let myself think about it, my stomach got all twisted up in a knot. Not knowin' a soul, not havin' a place to stay, not even knowin' if there were other Negroes, free or otherwise, livin' in town. I wasn't even sure if an old Negro woman like me could get a bed or a room. "The good Lord led you here, Clara," I told myself. "You better just stop your worryin' and leave everything up to Him."

COLONEL WADSWORTH: DENVER, COLORADO, JUNE 8, 1859

We left Leavenworth, Kansas, in April and reached Denver City on June 8. Took us nigh on eight weeks to cover 680 miles. Clara walked all the way, but then so did many of the others, the wagons being full of supplies and such. It's a hard way to travel. There ain't no doubt.

I was mighty glad to get to Denver. We drove into town, said our goodbyes, and then everyone went their separate ways, some continuing on into the mountains, others staying in town to set up businesses of their own. Mostly people wanted to take a few deep breaths and relax a little bit before they went off to live the rest of their lives!

CLARA

My goodness me, let me tell you, that first sight of Denver weren't no comfort. How could anyone think to call that a city? Now, St. Louis was a city, even Leavenworth was a city, but that tiny cluster of people was just the bare beginnings of a town. A few log cabins dotted the edge of the creek, some teepees huddled together on the other side of the river, and some businesses and professionals had set up shop, all in the shadow of the saloons and gambling houses.

HENRY REITZE

I met Clara when she came into my shop. I owned a bakery and restaurant. She came in for a meal. I noticed her right off because she was the first Negro woman I'd seen in town.

Clara needed a job and I needed someone to help me feed the swarms of hungry men that came here every day. Clara was a fine cook and we had much in common, mainly a love for the Lord and a desire, no, I'll say a passion, to share that love any way we knew how. For Clara, sharing came in the form of kind words, a cheerful smile, and a generous streak a mile wide. Wherever there was a poor soul in need, Clara was first in line to help.

CONCERNS ABOUT DENVER

Clara had good reason to wonder if she would be the only black woman in Denver. In the 1860 census, only 15 black men and 8 black women were listed as living in the area. By 1870 that number had increased to only 237.

CLARA

It didn't take me long to get settled and find a job. All that worry for nothin'. I guess I should have learned by now the Lord will provide.

Cookin' at City Bakery felt as natural as breathin'. After all, I been cookin' and cleanin' for other people my whole life, haven't I? And I liked workin' at City Bakery, too. So many of these men were without anyone to look after them, having left their mama or wife behind. I do believe that the good Lord wanted me to cook them up some good healthy eatin'. I counted

HAVE BIBLE, WILL TRAVEL

In the early days of the West, before churches were built, people's spiritual needs were met by traveling ministers. These strong and devoted men traveled from mining camp to mining camp preaching, performing weddings, and doing whatever else was needed. Winter, summer, spring, and fall found them carrying their belongings in forty- to fifty-pound packs on their backs, climbing steep mountains, walking great distances, and suffering through poor food and housing. The Reverend Jacob Adriance was such a man.

The clothing this African American woman is wearing is much like the clothing Clara had worn. Note the washboard in her left hand. Photo courtesy of the Denver Public Library Western History Colllection.

it a pleasure to try and put some meat back on their scrawny bones.

I only worked at City Bakery for a couple of months, and I spent most of my time cookin' in the back, but still, this here town is small and it didn't take long 'afore I got to know many of the people in it. Lordy, what an interestin' crowd. There were some who'd just as soon shoot you as look at you, while others would give you the shirt off'n their back or the hat off'n their head if they thought it might help. This here's the Wild West. No one ends up here by accident. None of these people was born in this town. They all came here hopin' to find somethin', or hopin' to get away from somethin' else. I guess that's why I got along so well with all these folks, 'cause I'm just like them—chasin' a dream and running from a nightmare.

REVEREND JACOB ADRIANCE,
METHODIST MINISTER:
AUGUST 1859
I can boast of being one of the first preachers to come to Denver—sent by the Methodist Church.

My job is to do the Lord's work and eventually establish a church here. Thankfully, I found a few devout souls in this heathen territory. Aunt Clara Brown was one.

When I got here, my first order of business was to find a place to live. Brother Reitze helped me rent a cabin about a block away from City Bakery. It was small, only one room, all of twelve feet by fourteen feet. It had a window and a door and a dirt floor. I've stayed in worse, and at least it's big enough to hold prayer meetings or to put up the occasional stranger that needs a place to stay.

Of course there were no church buildings here. I guess, in the building of a town the church always comes after the saloons, the general store, and the gambling halls. But I didn't need a church anyway. I intended to start having prayer meetings at my cabin as soon as I got settled.

CLARA

Lordy, Lordy, that Reverend Adriance was a godly man. Mmm, mmm, it felt good to go to

---

WHAT IS A GRUBSTAKE?

Prospectors, by necessity, carried all their supplies with them, usually taking enough to last at least thirty days up to the mountains.

When greenhorn miners came to the mining towns, they needed to buy all their food and supplies. This was an expensive investment. A common way to get around this was by being "grubstaked." This meant that an investor paid for part or all of a miner's supplies in exchange for a share of his profits. This was a risky investment, however, because most miners came back broke!

---

a prayer meetin' again. But Brother Adriance did more than pray. He put his words into action. That's what I liked about him. How many times did I see that poor, humble man invite strangers in to sleep on his floor and eat his food?

It didn't take me long to figure out a way to help. I told you I liked cookin'. Well, I just started overestimatin' how much an old colored gal like me could eat. When I cooked my dinner, I made more than enough and then some. Of course, I couldn't let all that good home cookin' go to waste, so I took the extra over to Reverend Adriance's house. Leastways, that's what I told him. I'm not sure if he believed me, but I know he was grateful for the help. Nothin' pleasures me more than seeing a hungry stomach bein' filled. The Reverend often said that he could preach the love of the Lord better to a full stomach than to an empty one.

REVEREND ADRIANCE

Clara was generous in so many ways. Not only did she help out with the care and feeding of many of the poor souls who passed through my house, but she offered up her own home to have prayer services. And when we started collecting money to build the church, Clara was as generous with her money as she was with her time. She wanted to see the love of God spread throughout the frontier. In fact, she attended the very first meeting on forming a nondenominational Sunday school. That was a good day for the up-and-coming city of Denver.

CLARA: SPRING 1860

I weathered a winter in Denver, but as soon as the snow began to melt, I headed even farther west into the mountains. It weren't no easy task gettin' myself up there, neither. I rode in a wagon with a friend, pretendin' to be his servant. It took us more'n a week to travel forty miles. I didn't mind. I enjoyed the scenery. I'd never been in the mountains before.

Another busy day along Central City's main street in 1864. Photo courtesy of the Denver Public Library Western History Collection.

I still hadn't given up on my dream of finding Eliza Jane. And besides, I knew that there was plenty of money to be made doin' laundry up at the diggin's. The miners work hard, day and night, thinking of nothing else but getting the gold outta them mountains.

Right away I found a little house, and as soon as I could find someone to make me a sign, I opened the first laundry in Gilpin County. Land sakes, what did they do with all of those dirty flannel shirts and long johns 'afore I came? I know I worked plenty hard sweatin' and strainin' over that steamin' hot laundry tub washin' 'em clean. But I didn't mind. Even when I was worn out from a long day on my feet, I was happy. Let me tell you. I's used to workin' just as hard for someone else. The ways I see it, hard work is a blessin' when you doin' it for yourself.

And the money was good, too. I charged fifty cents a shirt. I could buy me five loaves of bread with that fifty cents. And you know what? In the back of my mind I was doin' it for Eliza Jane, too. I never gave up hope of finding her. That hope was like my shadow. I took it with me everywhere. And when I saved money or bought more property or grubstaked another miner, I hoped that someday Eliza Jane would reap the reward.

Miner: Central City, Colorado, Summer 1860

Clara grubstaked me when I started out mining. In exchange for part ownership in my mine, she paid for my supplies, bought my food, and filled me with confidence that one day I would strike gold. And I did! I don't think anything gave me more pleasure than going back to Clara and paying her the money I owed her. Truth is, I owed Clara more than money. Thanks to her early confidence in me, I'm a rich man right now.

And I wasn't the only one she helped,

MORE ON BARNEY FORD

Barney Ford was an escaped slave. He planned to join the California Gold Rush in 1849, traveling by boat to San Francisco. During a stop in Nicaragua, he saw a business opportunity and stayed to open a hotel. His hotel did so well, he never continued on to California. He met Clara when he again tried his hand at mining, this time in Central City. Because he was black, he had to get a white lawyer to file the claim for him. Eventually, Barney was cheated out of his mine, but he returned to Denver and opened a string of successful businesses.

either. She didn't make a big deal about it, but Clara got a lot of us started. I know it was good business, but somehow I always felt that for her it was something more than business.

BARNEY FORD: CENTRAL CITY, COLORADO, FALL 1860

I met Clara when I went to her cabin up in Mountain City lookin' for a place to stay. I'd just come from Denver and planned on doing some mining. Clara let me stay at her house until I could find other arrangements. I enjoyed her company. We had something in common, 'cause I too had been a slave. I ran away from my owner in Carolina, and after many twists and turns of fate, I wound up here.

I admired Clara. I don't think a day went by when she wasn't doing good for someone. She delivered babies, nursed injured miners, and always found ways to give away her hard-earned money.

CLARA: SUMMER 1865

I worked hard, bought land when I had the chance, and can you believe that after livin' in these mountains for five years, I owned property worth $10,000? Praise the Lord! Who'da thought it?

Through it all, I never gave up on finding my little girl. I had friends write letters for me. I asked every person I met if they'd seen her. Every time a new colored person came into town, I'd go and say hello, hoping that maybe this might be the one who knew my Eliza Jane. Nothin' ever worked out, though, and I spent many a disappointed night mournin' the fact. There was just no word on Eliza Jane.

CLARA: SUMMER 1865

Praise the Lord. The Civil War done ended. Findin' that out was one of the happiest days of my life. President Lincoln gone and freed all the slaves. That meant my Eliza Jane was a free woman! I knew I had to go and find her. Besides, I was gettin' a hankerin' to go on back to Kentucky. I might be an old woman, but there is still a lot of spring left in this old hen.

Afterword

And that is exactly what Clara did. She went back to Kentucky, looking for her daughter. But she had no luck. Even though she didn't find Eliza Jane, she met many blacks who had been displaced by the Civil War. Many lived in extreme poverty, and many were eager to restart their life somewhere else. So Clara decided to help. She gathered together a group of sixteen ex-slaves and paid for them to come back to Colorado where she helped them find jobs and places to live.

As Clara grew older, she lost most of her money. Floods and fires wiped out records of some of her real estate holdings, and bringing the ex-slaves out west drained much of her savings. The long trip had tired her out, too, making it hard for her to keep up with the physically demanding job of doing laundry. Eventually, Clara had to move away from Central City. Her old friends got together and found a house where she could live in Denver rent-free. The citizens of Denver helped change the rules so that Clara could be considered a Colorado Pioneer and in this way receive a pension for the rest of her life. She was the first woman, and the first person of color, to be honored in this way.

Clara never gave up looking for Eliza Jane. And then, in 1882, she received the letter she'd been waiting for. A friend had located Eliza Jane in Iowa. Mother and daughter were reunited, and finally Clara could truly enjoy the many accomplishments of her long and fruitful life.

Bibliography

Asante, Molefi K., and Mark T. Mattson. *Historical and Cultural Atlas of African Americans.* New York: Macmillan Publishing, 1991.

Ballast, David Kent. *The Denver Chronicle: From a Golden Past to a Mile-High Future.* Houston, TX: Gulf Publishing, 1995.

Bruyn, Kathleen. *"Aunt" Clara Brown: Story of a Black Pioneer.* Boulder, CO: Pruett Publishing, 1971.

———. Papers, including letters and manuscript. Western History Department, Denver Public Library, Denver, CO.

Dorsett, Lyle W. *The Queen City: A History of Denver.* Boulder, CO: Pruett Publishing, 1977.

Hollenback, Frank R. *Central City and Black Hawk, Colorado—Then and Now.* Denver, CO: Sage Books, 1961.

Katz, William Loren. *Black Women of the West.* Rev. ed. New York: Anchor Press/Doubleday, 1973.

Patent, Dorothy Hinshaw. *West by Covered Wagon: Retracing the Pioneer Trails.* New York: Walker, 1995.

Schlissel, Lillian. *Black Frontiers: A History of African American Heroes in the Old West.* New York: Simon & Schuster, 1995.

Varnell, Jeanne. *Women of Consequence: The Colorado Women's Hall of Fame.* Boulder, CO: Johnson Books, 1999.

Margaret Brown

(1867–1932)

〰〰

Y OU PROBABLY ALREADY KNOW ABOUT MOLLY BROWN because of her famous trip on the *Titanic* in 1912. But did you know that in real life, Margaret Brown was never even called Molly? That was a name made up to tell the story of her life in the play *The Unsinkable Molly Brown*.

Margaret Brown did travel on the *Titanic*. She helped keep her fellow lifeboat passengers calm and focused on survival during their eight hours alone on the Atlantic. Then she spent the days following the disaster helping take care of the survivors. Margaret Brown returned home a heroine.

What you might not know is that by the time forty-five-year-old Margaret sailed on the *Titanic*, she'd already accomplished quite a lot. She was a tireless fundraiser, bringing in thousands of dollars for charity. She was largely self-educated, spending time and money relentlessly pursuing knowledge and self-improvement. And although she was a millionaire, she never forgot her family or her roots, proving to be a generous and trusted friend to all who knew her.

MRS. JOHANNA TOBIN: HANNIBAL, MISSOURI, 1886

Heartbroken. I was that sorry to say good-bye to my sweet daughter, Maggie. Sending her out into the world, a young woman off to the Wild West. Who could know what fearful troubles might befall her?

But her desire to leave Hannibal came as no surprise to me. Lively, ambitious Maggie needed more excitement in her life than she'd find here in Hannibal. "Go out and find a place for yourself in this world," I told her. Like

OPPOSITE: *This studio portrait of Margaret Brown was taken between 1900 and 1910. She is elegantly attired in one of her lavishly decorated evening gowns. Photo courtesy of the Denver Public Library Western History Collection.*

many young women, Maggie wanted adventure, but unlike so many, my red-headed darlin' had the courage to go and find it.

A TIGHT FIT

Margaret's family of eight lived only a few blocks away from the Mississippi River. Their house consisted of four rooms, a kitchen, a bedroom, a front room, and a larger basement room dug into the side of a hill.

MARGARET

I was nineteen and I knew what my life would be like if I stayed here. I'd marry a local boy, work hard raising and caring for a family, and finally, when my time was through, leave Hannibal feet first. I hoped for more out of life, and if there was more out there, then I intended to find it!

HELEN TOBIN, MARGARET'S SISTER

Our big brother, Daniel, moved to the mining town of Leadville, Colorado, hoping to make his fortune as a miner. A year later he sent Maggie and me the money for a train ticket. I went for a visit, but Maggie planned on staying in Leadville

This modest wood-frame house in Hannibal, Missouri, was Margaret Brown's childhood home. Photo courtesy of the Denver Public Library Western History Collection.

People, dogs, and burros share Harrison Avenue, Leadville's main street. This photograph was taken between 1900 and 1910. Photo courtesy of the Denver Public Library Western History Collection.

BOOMTOWN

Leadville got its start when silver was discovered there as early as 1870. By 1880, it was Colorado's second largest city. Miners, looking everywhere for the precious metal, burrowed into every nook and cranny possible. The hills surrounding the town were dotted with mines, and there were even mining tunnels under the town itself. In fact, residents had to be careful because it wasn't uncommon for a sinkhole to appear in somebody's backyard.

to keep house for Daniel. Yet I knew that there was another reason she wanted to go west. She told me on the train that she planned "to marry a rich man." That's what she said, but I knew that money wasn't all Maggie wanted. The West is wide open and full of possibilities. That is what was calling Maggie, the possibilities.

CLOUD CITY

Denver is nicknamed the Mile High City because it is one mile above sea level. Leadville is a mile higher than that. The city's elevation is 10,152 feet, almost two miles above sea level.

MARGARET: LEADVILLE, COLORADO, 1886

It's funny. No matter how much you want to start a new life, it's still hard to say good-bye to the old one. So many feelings I had about leaving. Sorrow when I looked back at Hannibal. Excitement when I looked forward to the future.

When we stepped from the train in Leadville, I saw a busy, bustling town. Harrison Avenue, Leadville's main street, was packed full with men and mammals. Freight wagons, mule trains, and horse-drawn carriages clogged the street. Men in dusty, worn-out prospector clothing shared the wooden sidewalks with respectable-looking businessmen and fancy-dressed dancehall girls. The air vibrated with the braying of donkeys, the neighing of horses, and the yelling of men telling them to be quiet. The hiss and whistle of the train wove in between the tinkly, tinny piano music drifting out of the saloons.

WHEN'S THE FUN START?

The cost of living in Leadville was high. Between the two of them, Margaret and Daniel could barely make ends meet. Daniel made about $60 a month working in the mine. Margaret, being a woman, probably made only half that working at the store. Grocery costs were high. For instance, a sack of flour cost about $3.50, a pound of potatoes 4¢, and a can of milk 30¢. Boardinghouses at the time charged anywhere from $7 to $15 per month, and Daniel and Margaret paid more than that because they rented a house

Right away, I felt the energy and excitement that filled Leadville's streets. Right away, I was glad I came.

DANIEL
Margaret and Helen, looking fresh-faced and wholesome as they stepped off that train, found me grinning from ear to ear. True, I lived with my sister Catherine and her husband, but there were a whole lot more Tobins in Hannibal than in Leadville. I missed my family. I missed my home.

MARGARET
Daniel and I rented a house. He worked hard as a day miner, getting three dollars for a ten- to twelve-hour shift. He came home bone weary and dirty from head to toe. The money he made didn't cover all of our expenses. I found a job working at Daniels, Fisher and Smith, a fancy department store. I sewed draperies, carpet, and shades. I didn't mind the work though. After all, I've had a job since I turned thirteen and got out of school.

A MAN OF POTENTIAL

J. J. Brown was born in 1854 in Pennsylvania to immigrant parents. At the age of twenty-three, he left home, seeking his fortune as a miner. As most miners do, he moved around quite a bit, spending time in the Black Hills of South Dakota and the Aspen area of Colorado before settling down in Leadville. During that time, he picked up some of the extensive knowledge and mining expertise that eventually brought him his fortune.

J. J. BROWN: EARLY SUMMER 1886
I'll always remember the first day I saw Margaret, her head thrown back laughing, her red hair shining in the sun. That broad smile and vivacious energy beckoned me like a moth to a flame. She might not have been the prettiest girl at that church picnic, but to my eyes, there was no one else worth looking at. I decided right then and there to ask her out.

MARGARET
Even in a city like Leadville, made up mostly of men, J. J. (Jim) Brown stood out. Tall and handsome, Irish and Catholic, he had the reputation of a charmer. I never imagined a thirty-one-year-old man of the world like J. J. Brown would be interested in me.

Jim worked as a shift manager at the mine. He seemed just like most of the other men in town, but once I got to know him, I saw a difference. Ambitious and intelligent, he loved mining. He wanted to learn everything about it. At night, after ten hours under the mountain, he came home and read about geology, mining techniques, and whatever else he could find.

JIM BROWN: SUMMER 1886

Right away, I got permission to call on Miss Margaret Tobin. It didn't take long for Maggie to show her true colors. I arrived at her house, hat in hand, full of plans for our first evening together. When she came to the door, Maggie looked past me to my rather shabby one-horse carriage parked in the street. "No, thank you," she said and walked inside.

Margaret Tobin didn't consent to a seat by my side until I came back the next evening driving a much nicer, two-horse carriage. Only nineteen years old, and yet, she knew exactly what she wanted and wouldn't accept less. I liked that.

MARGARET

I knew what I wanted and Jim wasn't it. I wanted to marry a rich man and Jim wasn't rich—not even close. I wanted to marry someone to help me give my parents some of the luxuries they'd missed working day and night to keep us six children in that tiny house, with food on the table and shoes on our feet.

But it didn't take long for me to fall in love with Mr. J. J. Brown, a poor, hard-working miner. I tried to resist, but finally I figured I'd be happier marrying for love than money.

So I married Jim. When I became Mrs. J. J. Brown, I stopped cooking and caring for my brother, moved into my husband's tiny house, and began cooking and caring for him.

THOMAS CAHILL: 1887

I worked with Margaret at the Daniels, Fisher and Smith Department Store before she got married. I hated to see her quit her job, but it wasn't proper for married ladies to work.

Margaret and Jim moved up to Stumpftown, a tiny community a few miles out of Leadville, which brought them closer to Jim's work at the mine. They lived in a two-room cabin. Margaret hauled water from the one well in town.

Happy were the days when I made a delivery from Daniels, Fisher and Smith to Margaret's cabin. She greeted me with a warm smile and a big piece of homemade cake or pie. We visited at the kitchen table. Margaret dearly loved to hear the news of her old friends at the department store.

JIM

Once we got married, Margaret started taking lessons with a private tutor. She wanted to improve herself and she loved to learn. After all of her work at the house was done, she traveled to Leadville and took lessons in reading and literature, three hours a day, five days a week. Now that's what I call determination. She also took piano and singing lessons. Maybe I should have taken notice of how much Margaret loved to perform, even back then.

MARGARET

You might have heard a famous story about me. The story goes that Jim struck it rich and brought the money home, asking me to hide it. I stuck it in the iron cookstove and went to bed. The tale goes on to say that Jim came home none the better for a night out celebrating. When he lit the fire, *POOF!* Our just-found fortune went up in smoke. Of course, I cried and cried and cried until Jim told me not to worry. Then he went out and found himself another fortune—just like that. What a hoot!

It's a good story, don't you think? I laugh every time I hear it, even more so when I'm the one doing the telling.

JIM

Hmph! How can that woman let people tell such lies about her? The truth of that story isn't nearly as colorful as one of Margaret's fabrications. It's true,

Twenty-four-year-old Margaret Brown poses with her husband, J. J., and their two children, Helen and Lawrence. Photo courtesy of the Colorado Historical Society.

WE HAD A BALL!

Fancy dress balls were one way that Leadville residents had fun. An annual event of the season was the Hard Times Ball. Admission to the dance cost 99¢. Men dressed in their miners' outfits while the women came in everyday house dresses. This way, even the poorest Leadville resident could enjoy a night out on the town.

one night I brought some money home, but it was from the office, about fifty dollars in gold coins in a metal box. I hid it in the stove for safekeeping. We forgot all about it and started a fire. The coins got hot, and I had to let them cool off before I took them back to work. That's the end of the story. Nothing fancy, just the plain old truth.

MARY, THE BROWNS' HOUSEKEEPER

Ah, workin' for the Browns was a dream come true, don'tcha know. They hired me to help with the housework and to take care of those precious babies of theirs. Lawrence was born in 1887 and Helen in 1889. I liked working for Mrs. Brown. She treated me like a regular person, not hired help, if you know what I mean.

The Browns loved to entertain and be entertained, and not a nicer, more generous couple you'll ever meet. Their house was always full of people coming and going. They usually had at least one relative staying with them, and often Mrs. Brown's parents were living there, too.

I looked after the wee ones while Mrs. Brown did her charity work, throwing herself headfirst

STRIKING GOLD

Over the years, Jim gradually became known as one of the best mining men in Leadville. In 1891, several prominent Leadville businessmen formed the Ibex Mining Company and hired Jim to oversee their mining operation. In this capacity, he figured out how to change the Little Jonny Mine from a silver to a gold mine. Jim began drilling and almost immediately ran into a slippery layer of sand that made it impossible to continue drilling the shaft. Most people urged him to give up, saying it would be too expensive to fix this problem. Using cheap bales of hay and huge timbers, Jim was able to hold back the sand and thus find his pot of gold.

into her work. No organizing church picnics for her. Mrs. Brown had other, bigger ideas in mind. She organized soup kitchens and helped feed the poor folks in Leadville. Not a small task, let me tell you. It took a lot of work and even more energy. And Mrs. Brown didn't just boss people around, either. No, she was always in the middle of things, with her sleeves rolled up doing her part. It made me tired just watchin' her. Didn't seem to mind the work, though. I guess she just liked doing for others.

MARGARET
When I look back now, those early years in Leadville were truly the good old days, the best days really, with Jim and I working together to build our life and our family. Jim and I liked each other back then. The money and travel and different lifestyles hadn't come between us yet. My outspoken ways didn't bother him much, and I tolerated his Irish temper.

JIM
Indoors or outdoors, summer, winter, spring, or fall, Leadville offered plenty to do. I think I loved the winter parties the best. Gliding along in a sleigh pulled by six high-stepping horses, Margaret and I snuggled under a buffalo robe. Sometimes we headed up to Twin Lakes for an afternoon of ice-skating, which always included frozen feet, hot chocolate, and lots and lots of laughter.

MARGARET

I married a poor man for love, but lucky me, that poor man struck it rich. By October 1893, Jim had worked his way up to superintendent of the Ibex Mining Company, running all their mines. Once the price of silver fell, they decided to go back into some of the old silver mines looking for gold. The Little Jonny was one such mine. There were naysayers aplenty telling Jim that it couldn't be done, but as usual, Jim didn't listen to anyone but himself.

JIM: OCTOBER 1893

My determination paid off. I struck gold—big! In fact, that vein was so rich, one expert said it looked like a *lake* of ore. The Ibex Mining Company said their thanks with shares in the company and a place on the board. All of a sudden, Margaret and I were millionaires!

MARGARET

Can you image going to bed poor and waking up a millionaire? That's what happened to me. My life changed overnight. All of a sudden, the door to the world opened wide and I couldn't wait to step through it. We wanted to celebrate, so the family set off to see the States.

We got back to Leadville in time to celebrate Christmas. I knew that it would be my last one here. The town was just too small to hold me now.

UPTOWN GIRL

It is generally believed that Margaret Brown was snubbed by Denver society. This isn't true. She was snubbed by Mrs. Crawford Hill, the queen of society, for not being good enough to join in her circle of friends, the most elite, richest group in Denver social circles. Many other prominent citizens were also snubbed. As Kristen Iversen explains in her book, *Molly Brown: Unraveling the Myth*, "In 1894 to the early 1920s, the Browns took up more space in Denver's society pages than nearly any other Denver family and were regularly listed on the Social Register. Margaret and J. J. were not ostracized from Denver society—they were Denver society."

Mary, Daniel's Wife: Spring 1894

Margaret and Jim left Leadville for Denver. It seems that all of the people who strike it rich leave. But thanks to the Browns' generosity, their success was our success, too. Jim put Daniel in charge of the day-to-day operations of running his company.

Margaret: Denver, Colorado, April 1894

We moved to Denver and soon found the house we wanted to buy. A beautiful, three-story red-brick house at 1340 Pennsylvania. It had all the most modern conveniences: central heating, electrical wiring, plumbing, and a hand-crank telephone. From my front porch I saw the city, and far beyond that the mountains. We were right smack-dab in the middle of things, in the very best of neighborhoods.

After we moved in, a spring snowfall blanketed the streets. We celebrated our new house and our new life by driving our sleigh up and down Pennsylvania, singing Irish songs at the top of our lungs.

Mrs. Crawford Hill, Society Matron: April 1894

These Irish mining wives have no family background, are ill bred, and have no sense of style. They make it rich and want to be included in proper society. Well, that is just *not* how it's done. Just because Margaret Brown lived in the right neighborhood doesn't mean Margaret Brown was the right kind of person. She was Irish and Catholic after all, hardly two traits that recommended her to my company. No. Of course, Mrs. James J. Brown could not be included in the activities of the Sacred Thirty-six.

SHE'S SO PRETTY

In those days, putting photographs in newspapers was so expensive that it was rarely done. Instead, newspapers used sketches of an outfit or very detailed descriptions. In this way, readers could actually picture the dress in their minds and perhaps even copy it without the aid of a photo.

Margaret

Who said I needed Mrs. Crawford Hill's approval to make it in "society?" I met the right people just fine without her.

Helen: Spring 1894

Soon after we moved to Denver, Mother and Father bought property out of town, near the foothills along Bear Creek. They built a beautiful house that they named Avoca. We spent our summers there. Daddy raised chickens, Mother had fabulous parties, and Lawrence and I drove our pony cart wherever we wanted. Friends took the train out from Denver. We hunted, fished, and explored along the river. It was heavenly.

Seventeenth Street, Denver, 1900. Photo courtesy of the Library of Congress.

JIM: 1900

In her typical style, Margaret pushed her way right into the middle of Denver society. A genius at organizing charity functions, she created quite a stir with her energy and enthusiasm. Boy, could she raise the money. Thanks to Margaret's efforts, wings were added on to hospitals, churches were built, poor children were fed and clothed, and wounded or sick soldiers were cared for. Let me tell you, Denver society never saw anything like Margaret. The parties she organized were unbelievable—the social events of the season. Margaret never did anything halfway.

Margaret's charity work cost me a fortune. Those fancy parties of hers required fancy dresses, which of course meant gowns from Paris. Women all over Denver watched, read about, and then copied what Margaret wore to her parties.

DENVER RESIDENT

I couldn't wait to read the newspapers every day. I turned right to the society pages. My husband grumbled about those "rich snobs," but that's exactly why I liked readin' about them. Gave me a break from cookin', cleanin', and wipin' runny noses. My favorite person to read about was Mrs. J. J. Brown. I liked her because she started out "just plain folks," like me. What a life! More like a fairy tale, really. She was always doing something glamorous, goin' to plays or the opera, or having friends over to a simple, fifteen-course dinner party!

The Denver Times: DECEMBER 6, 1900

"One of the most brilliantly attractive and richly gowned women was Mrs. J. J. Brown. Her hair was dressed in a quaintly artistic fashion, built high and finished with a gilt snake coiled about an aigrette in which glittered two large solitaires and a cluster of opals and diamonds. Two long curls, of the sort that don't repose on the toilet table at night, fell over her beautiful bare shoulders. Her gown was just imported from Venice and the artistic touches of the clever modiste were apparent in every detail."

LEADVILLE RESIDENT: 1900

In my opinion, the real mark of a lady is how she treats people. Let me tell you, Margaret Brown was a lady, all right. Long after the Browns made their

Portrait of Margaret Brown. Photo courtesy of the Library of Congress.

fortune, Margaret still visited Leadville. She never acted uppity or in one little bit changed, just 'cause she had money and we didn't. I loved seeing her because Margaret was full of fun. She always acted real glad to see all of her old friends, and I can tell you, we were all real glad to see her.

JIM: DECEMBER 1900

I never understood that woman and I'm sure I never will. Always moving, organizing, or gallivanting around the world. Why did she do that? And why did Helen need to go to a fancy school in Paris? Why couldn't Lawrence attend school in Colorado? And above all, why did she think she needed to go back to college? She proved herself long ago.

MARGARET

Jim never understood that I went back to college for myself. I've always loved to learn, even back in Leadville when I jumped at the chance to go to that tutor. When a fine school like the Carnegie Institute first opened its doors to women, you can bet that I wanted to be there to take advantage of it. I am determined to be the best that I can be. Life is too big and holds too much promise to sit back and watch it go by.

≈ *Afterword* ≈

Margaret continued to live her life to the fullest. Gradually, she and Jim grew apart. Perhaps Margaret was too independent and outspoken for him. She traveled more and more, making friends with rich and famous people from all over the world. As she grew older, her list of accomplishments grew. Margaret was awarded the French Legion of Honor for her service in World War I. She got involved in politics, running unsuccessfully for a seat in the Senate. And she pursued her dream of acting, taking classes from one of the world's most famous actresses, Sarah Bernhardt.

Margaret Tobin Brown was a woman who used her energy and money to improve the lives of countless others. She was a woman not afraid to take a risk or speak her mind. Most of all, she was a woman who stayed true to herself and followed her heart.

≈ *Bibliography* ≈

Benzinger, James George. "Memories of a Grandson." Family papers and correspondence. Molly Brown House Museum, Denver.

Blair, Edward. *Leadville: Colorado's Magic City*. Boulder, CO: Pruett Publishing, 1980.

Brackney, Charles. "Remembering Molly." *Denver Post*. April 13, 1997, 10–20.

Brown, Margaret Tobin. Family papers and correspondence Clipping file. Molly Brown House Museum, Denver.

Iversen, Kristen. *Molly Brown: Unraveling the Myth*. Boulder, CO: Johnson Books, 1999.

Ubbeholde, Carl, Maxine Benson, and Duane A. Smith. *A Colorado History*. Boulder, CO: Pruett Publishing, 1972.

Varnell, Jeanne. *Women of Consequence*. Boulder, CO: Johnson Books, 1999.

Whitacre, Christine. *Molly Brown: Denver's Unsinkable Lady*. Denver: Historic Denver, 1993.

Nellie Cashman

(1844–1925)

❧

NELLIE CASHMAN WAS BORN IN COUNTY CORK, IRELAND, in 1844. Like more than 900,000 other Irish immigrants in the 1850s and 1860s, Nellie and her family fled the poverty and starvation of Ireland in the hope of starting a new life in the United States. In 1860, her family arrived in Boston, where Nellie found work as a servant. Then, when she was twenty-five, Nellie moved west with her sister, Fannie. They settled in San Francisco.

Although Fanny soon married, Nellie was too restless to stay in one place for long. She moved from one mining town to another, hoping to find her fortune, but always enjoying her freedom along the way. Not afraid of hard work, long hours, or people's opinions of how a woman should act, Nellie approached life in her own way, on her own terms.

MINER: CASSIAR, BRITISH COLUMBIA, 1877

The first time I met Miss Nellie Cashman, she was heading into the Cassiar District, one of the remotest places on this earth you could ever imagine. She signed on to cook for a party of us prospectors. When I saw her, I chuckled to myself, thinking this here woman ain't gonna be able to make the treacherous trip, slogging through snow up to her knees, day after day, living in a tent, carrying her own supplies. Why, even some of the strongest men had to turn back, and she was just a little bit of a woman, only five feet tall, and I bet she didn't weigh one hundred pounds soakin' wet. Pretty, too. With her fair Irish skin and her thick, dark hair all piled up on her head, she

OPPOSITE: *Nellie Cashman's independence, generosity, and business ability proved she was more than just a pretty face. Photo courtesy of the Denver Public Library Western History Collection.*

looked like a real lady. And when she spoke, with her liltin' Irish brogue, it sounded like music to my ears. I was wrong about her, let me tell you. Outside, she might have looked like a dainty little lady, but inside she had the heart and courage of a giant.

NELLIE: CASSIAR DISTRICT, 1877

It makes me laugh the way these men go on so; they always have, wherever I go and whoever I meet. These rough mountain-mining, backcountry men do carry on. They sound like nothing more than lovesick puppies. And speaking of love, that trip to the Cassiar was when I got my first real taste of prospecting, and I loved it. When we got there, I opened a boardinghouse, but whenever I could, I went out and did my own prospecting. I learned a lot. The miners were always willing to teach me what I didn't know. I liked it up there. Who knows, if that mine hadn't played out, I might be up there still.

MINER

I bless the day I met Miss Nellie. She was a true friend. And you know what she did? She done saved my life, that's what. After a full summer of prospecting and running her boardinghouse, she traveled back down to Victoria. When she got there, she heard that the miners she left behind, me included, were in bad shape...dying from scurvy. Well, if that woman didn't just turn around and head back our way with a load of supplies. Now, that might not seem like much to you, but would you be willing to risk your life and walk through eleven weeks of waist-high snow and freezing temperatures to help out a friend? Miss Nellie did. There ain't nothing I wouldn't do for that woman, and that's the truth as sure as I'm standing here today.

TRAVELING TO CANADA

Cassiar is in the eastern province of British Columbia, Canada. It is located in the northeast, very close to the Yukon Territory. Nellie traveled there with a group of other miners. In 1877, wearing men's pants, boots and a fur hat, she was the first white woman to lay eyes on this pristine, uninhabited wilderness.

NELLIE

Yes, I did save their lives, but I don't think I did anything all that extraordinary. I heard that some of my friends were in trouble, and

I went back to help. That is exactly what I've been doing all my life and what I aim to continue doing as long as the good Lord leaves me here on this earth…helping those in need. And I count myself lucky that I had the money and the strength to do it.

MINER

I was downright sorry to see Miss Nellie leave. I understood, though. The need for adventure and the need to see new sights just sort of gets in your blood. She had to move on. We call it "itchy feet." Her feet were itchin' to try out new roads. So I wished her the best and sorely hoped that our paths would cross again in this lifetime.

NELLIE: YUMA, ARIZONA, 1879

I took a stagecoach south to see what California had to offer. We bumped along trails until we came to Los Angeles. I didn't like it there, not even one little bit. So I continued on into Yuma, Arizona. Such a place. Hot and dry and dusty. It was swarming with bugs, although why a bug would want to live there, I can't even begin to imagine. We set down to eat our dinner: beans, the usual fare of the road. I asked the driver, very politely mind you, if he hadn't seasoned the beans with a little too much pepper.

STAGECOACH DRIVER

I just about laughed my head off when Miss Cashman asked me that. You get to know people pretty well when you travel with them

HOW CAN I HELP?

Nellie assembled a group of six men and traveled back to Cassiar with 1,500 pounds of supplies, much of it potatoes. They traveled for seventy-seven days, walking on snowshoes through deep snow and camping out in frigid winter weather. Nellie pulled some of the supplies on a sled behind her, never asking for or expecting help from the men in her group.

I'LL BE GOOD, I PROMISE

Yuma became famous for its "modern" territorial prison, built in 1876. The prisoners themselves helped build the stone and adobe structure, sometimes having to withstand 120-degree summer temperatures to get the job done. If inmates didn't behave, they faced being thrown in a scorpion-infested dungeon.

under such harsh conditions, and I knew that Miss Nellie Cashman was no stranger to hardship. Not a complainer, either. She was able to buck up under the worst of conditions. But when she asked me so politely about the pepper, I just about bust a gut. "That's not pepper, my friend," I said between gulps of laughter. "Those little black spots you see are mosquitoes. And if you're as hungry as I am, you'll eat them. Maybe they'll even add a little extra flavor." We ate those beans, bugs and all, and I enjoyed them more for the pretty company that I kept.

NELLIE: TUCSON, ARIZONA, 1879

From Yuma, I continued on to Tucson. Not much more there than a fort. The pace of Tucson was as slow as molasses in January. I opened a restaurant, called Delmonicos, and was making a success of it. But it didn't take me long to figure out that Tucson was not my cup of tea.

When I started looking around for someplace a little more interesting, my eyes turned to Tombstone, Arizona. They'd just discovered silver there, and I knew a boomtown when I saw one. True, Tombstone had a reputation for being a bit on the wild side, but that didn't scare me at all. I have spent the last ten years around the rawest and wildest of men and haven't once had cause for concern.

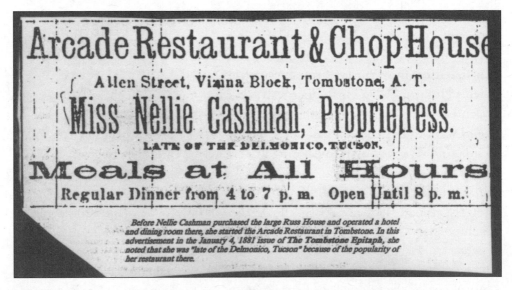

A savvy businesswoman, Nellie knew the importance of advertising. This ad, found in the January 4, 1881, issue of The Tombstone Epitaph *refers to an early business venture in Tombstone. Photo courtesy of the Arizona Historical Society, Tucson.*

John Clum, Editor of *The Tombstone Epitaph*: 1880

The day that Miss Nellie Cashman came to Tombstone was a glorious day indeed. Our growing city needed people that knew how to run a respectable business, and hadn't Miss Nellie proved herself time and time again? Why, she was a natural-born businesswoman. At first she opened a store, but soon figured that she might be better off running a restaurant. She did the advertising in this very paper. She charged double the going price for a meal, but I never heard any complaints. And besides, when a customer couldn't pay, Miss Nellie let them eat for free. She couldn't stand to see anyone suffering. I tell you, a softer heart you never did see.

Nellie: Tombstone, Arizona, 1880

Mr. John Clum and everyone else in Tombstone knew that I charged more than the going rate because I served a better meal than anyone else in town. As I said in my ads, the Russ House served "the best food this side of Pecos." And besides that, people eating in my establishment could rest assured that there were no cockroaches in my kitchen and the flour was free of bugs. That was more than you could say about some of the other restaurants in town!

Store Owner

Miss Nellie was always up to something good. I always knew when I saw her marching into my store that she was coming 'round asking for money for some charity or another. Don't get me wrong, I didn't mind a wink. After all, it wasn't so long ago that I was on the receiving end of her charity. It was more than once that she sat me down in her restaurant and filled my too-long-empty belly

NOW THAT'S WHAT I CALL GOOD GRUB

If you visited Nellie's restaurant on Sunday, November 8, 1881, you'd have to choose from such main course dishes as Beef a l'Espanol, Chicken Fricasse a la Crème, Stuffed Lamb, or Calf Head in Tortue. And you'd probably want to save some room for dessert of grapes and walnuts.

IS THIS A CHURCH?

Until Nellie could get her church built, she persuaded Wyatt Earp and the other owners of the infamous Crystal Saloon to allow church services to be held there.

Nellie never did have any problem with the town's seedier citizens. She often went and asked the saloon girls for money for her causes and found them to be more generous than their more righteous sisters. As for the desperadoes, Nellie had this to say: "The farther away you go from civilization, the bigger hearted and more courteous you find the men."

with food. Starting over in a new town is hard, mighty hard. But knowing people like Miss Nellie made it a whole lot easier.

FATHER GALLAGHER

Nellie thought that Tombstone needed a Catholic church, her being such a devout Catholic and all. Not one to wait around for someone else to take the lead, she talked to the powers that be and they agreed that if she raised the money to build a church, they'd get the priest. I chuckle whenever I hear this story, because they gave Nellie the hardest job. Imagine raising money for a church in a hard-nosed western town like Tombstone! But she did it. Raised seven hundred dollars just by asking people to donate money, which might not seem difficult, but you go and try to ask people to part with their hard-earned money and see how much you get. That seven hundred dollars was a direct result of people's high esteem for Miss Cashman.

Still, seven hundred dollars doesn't build a church. So Nellie got creative. She organized fund-raisers, including Tombstone's first amateur theater production and a grand ball. In short order, Nellie accomplished the job she set out to do, and ground was broken for Sacred Heart Catholic Church. I was sent to be the priest in the church that Nellie paid for. We've been good friends ever since.

JOHN CLUM

It's true. Nellie was always asking for something. But if she asked, we gave. When she needed actors for those gosh-darn plays of hers, we volunteered to be actors. And we had fun doing it, too. If she sold tickets for a fancy dress ball, we bought them, and then attended the ball in our best boots, cleanest clothes, and biggest smiles. You see, Nellie's good deeds not only helped those in need. She brought culture and fun to Tombstone. I always had something to write about in my newspaper when Nellie was around.

Nellie

I have one regret about those early days in Tombstone. Between business and my social causes, I had precious little time for prospecting. I always kept my ears open, though, and I made it a point to listen to the miners who came into my restaurant. During those days, I kept my hand in it by grubstaking those men lucky enough to be going out with a pick and shovel. It was a good deal for both of us. I furnished the food and supplies, they did the work, and we split the profits in half.

I saw other men in my restaurant besides miners, though. Some of the West's most famous desperadoes and lawmen passed through Tombstone. I suppose they came because the reputation of this city was known far and wide. But whatever the reason, I can tell you that even the most unruly and dangerous of men always acted like perfect gentlemen around me.

Doc Holliday

Ain't no reason not to act like a perfect gentleman. Nellie Cashman was as fine a woman as you'd ever want to meet. Pretty as a picture and her Irish brogue tickled my ears like fine piano music. I could have listened to her talk all day if'n she'da let me.

One day, as I was partaking of a fine meal in her restaurant, a particularly rude man complained about the quality of the food.

Nellie

Doc overheard his complaints and real slow like drew out his gun and pointed it at the man. "What did you say about Miss Nellie's food, mister?" he drawled.

The man, turning five shades of white, was at least smart enough to say respectfully, "Food's delicious. Good as I've ever tasted."

John Henry "Doc" Holliday looking more like a dentist than a desperado. Photo courtesy of the Denver Public Library Western History Collection.

DENTIST DESPERADO

Before he was a famous desperado, Doc Holliday was a dentist from Georgia. His real name was John Henry Holliday. He had tuberculosis and came west for his health. Doc welcomed gunfights because he said he didn't want to die in bed. Too bad. He ultimately died in Glenwood Springs at the ripe old age of thirty-six. He died in bed.

Doc just smiled as he put his revolver back into his holster. "Yep, that's what I thought you said."

Although I shouldn't, I laugh whenever I think of that story. My goodness, that poor customer could not have picked a worse time to complain.

Fanny, Nellie's Sister: San Francisco, California, Late 1880

My husband, Thomas Cunningham, died of tuberculosis, leaving me with five young children. I don't mind admitting that I was scared. Didn't think I could make enough money to feed my family, what with me being sick, too. I didn't know what to do. Of course, I sent for Nellie. She's always been a tower of strength. Just being around her made me feel better.

Nellie

My poor, poor sister and those five fatherless babies...the thought of them just made my heart break. Of course, there was nothing to think about—I had to help. I took off for San Francisco. I hadn't been there long before I realized that I'd have a much better chance taking care of my kin back in Tombstone. So we packed up the house and the children and headed back to Arizona. We were a family of seven. With this many mouths to feed, I needed to get right to work.

Fanny: Tombstone, Arizona, 1881

The climate of Arizona improved my health. Soon I was helping Nellie. Together we cleaned up and redecorated the Russ boardinghouse. We renamed it the American Hotel. Things were finally looking up.

You can imagine how heartbroken I was, then, when only about a month after opening the hotel, a fire swept through the business district of Tombstone.

Nellie and I and a few friends formed a bucket brigade. We worked and worked and worked to keep that boardinghouse from catching fire. I wasn't about to see all of my new dreams go up in smoke. Three times the building caught fire, and three times, through sheer grit and determination, we were able to put it out. After it was all over, part of the American Hotel and many of our belongings had been destroyed.

John Clum

Once again, Nellie showed her business smarts. A fire wasn't going to bring her to her knees. The damage was estimated at fifteen hundred dollars—a huge sum of money. But Nellie didn't have to waste a second worrying about finding the money to make the repairs. She'd insured the hotel for twice that amount.

Mike Cunningham, Nellie's Nephew: October 26, 1881

Living with Aunt Nellie in Tombstone proved to be an exciting adventure. One of the most exciting things was the knowledge that gunfights were bound to break out around town at any time. A famous gunfight, one you've probably heard about, was the shoot-out at the O.K. Corral. I didn't see the actual fight, but I was coming home from school when I came across the dying and wounded lying right there in the street. I watched the injured men get loaded onto flatbed wagons, and I heard their cries of pain. It was a sorry sight and one I'll never forget as long as I live.

FIRE!

Fire was a frequent problem in old-time boomtowns—the houses were made mostly of wood. It wasn't unusual for a boomtown to burn almost completely to the ground. In his newspaper, John Clum described the fire this way: "The blackened walls and smoking ruins of what was once handsome and beautiful buildings is all that remains of what was the very heart of Tombstone."

SHOOT-OUT AT THE O.K. CORRAL

The shoot-out at the O.K. corral was a famous old-time-Western draw-your-gun-in-the-middle-of-the-street gunfight. The Earp brothers and Doc Holliday, fighting on the good side of the law, battled three outlaws and won.

Nellie: Spring 1883

One day, a Mexican miner came into the Russ House and paid for his food with gold nuggets. He didn't speak much English, but I did make out that he got them out of a mine in Baja, California. Now, my feet were getting pretty itchy by that time, and a trip to California sounded appealing—and those gold nuggets looked mighty beautiful. Things seemed pretty much under control at home, so I got a group together and we headed out. We took the stage to Mexico and then a boat across the Gulf of California. We bought burros and equipment in Santa Rosalia before we crossed the desert. The trip was a bust. We got lost and almost died of thirst. I went for help and luckily stumbled on a priest who loaned me his mules and gave me some water to take back to the men. We barely made it back to civilization alive and in one piece. And although we came back poorer than we left, I don't regret a day of it. Life is too short not to go after your dreams.

Fanny

The children liked living in Tombstone. There was always plenty of excitement. Nellie was as kind and generous as she could be. She fed, clothed, and loved all my little ones as if they were her own.

Nellie

Being an aunt was a treat. My nephew Mike was the dickens, though, always getting into trouble. Once, he and a friend decided to go out and do some prospecting on their own. They loaded up their burros and headed out of town. Now, this might not have been such a bad idea, except that around Tombstone, the Apache Indians were still a problem. It wasn't safe leaving town, and Mike knew that. But, when the prospecting bug bites, you throw caution to the wind. Don't I know that! Anyway, lucky for Mike, a friend saw those two foolhardy boys head out of town and came to tell me. They got a head start on me. But I hitched up my buggy. By the time I found them, it was dark and the glow of the Apache campfires dotted the darkness. I found them shaking in their boots, huddled in a corner of an abandoned miner's house. I didn't know whether to hug Mike or spank him. I did the first, although I admit I considered the second.

MIKE

It didn't take my friends and I long to figure out that Aunt Nell was a soft touch. We played baseball in the vacant lot near home. When playing gave way to fighting, Aunt Nell heard the loud voices and came out to smooth things over. After giving us a long lecture, she'd bring us all a big piece of pie to sweeten our sour tempers. That pie was so tasty that pretty soon my friends and I were faking fights just to get another piece.

NELLIE: 1884

I thought my heart would break in half when my beautiful sister died of tuberculosis. We'd been through so much together, growing up in Ireland, traveling to a new country to start afresh in Boston, and then again in San Francisco. I thought living in Tombstone might just save her. But it didn't, and now her five children are orphans. But they have me, and I'll take care of them 'til the day I die.

Seventy-year-old Nellie Cashman, still looking stylish. Photo courtesy of the Arizona Historical Society, Tucson.

≈ *Afterword* ≈

Nellie did take care of her five nieces and nephews. She loved them and looked over them like a mother, putting them through school and visiting them often when they grew up.

By 1887, the silver mines in Tombstone had flooded, and just as quickly as Tombstone became a boomtown, it went bust. Nellie, with six mouths to feed, had to move on. She spent the next part of her life following the gold rush from boomtown to boomtown, opening restaurants or boardinghouses wherever she went. When the children grew up and no longer needed her care, she moved to Dawson, Alaska, where she spent the last twenty years of her life. She is reported to have made several fortunes mining. Wherever she went, Nellie earned money and then used it to help those in need.

❧ Bibliography ❧

Clum, John P. "Nellie Cashman." *Arizona Historical Review* 3 (October 1931): 9–35.

Ledbetter, Suzann. *Nellie Cashman: Prospector and Trailblazer.* El Paso: Texas Western Press, 1993.

Mayer, Melanie J. *Klondike Women: True Tales of the 1897–98 Gold Rush.* Columbus: Swallow Press/Ohio Univ. Press, 1989.

McLoone, Margo. *Women Explorers in North and South America.* Mankato, MN: Capstone Press, 1997.

Reiter, Joan Swallow. *The Old West: The Women.* Alexandria, VA: Time-Life Books, 1978.

Rochlin, Harriet. "The Amazing Adventures of a Good Woman." *Journal of the West* 12 (April 1973): 281–95.

Seagraves, Anne. *High-Spirited Women of the West.* Hayden, ID: Wesanne Publications, 1992.

Sarah Winnemucca

(1844–1891)

〰〰

Sarah Winnemucca, a Northern Paiute Indian from northern Nevada, was born on the edge of change. In a short span of time, she lived through the settling of a wilderness and the destruction of a way of life her people had known for centuries.

Sarah's grandfather, Captain Truckee, was a significant figure in her childhood. He told a story that shaped her future:

At the beginning of time, the Great Spirit lived with his four children. These children, a dark-skinned boy and girl and a light-skinned boy and girl, never seemed to get along. They fought and bickered until finally the Great Spirit separated them. He sent the light-skinned children far away, but promised that one day they would return to live in harmony with their dark-skinned brothers.

SARAH: NEVADA, 1844

I was born in the year 1844 near Humboldt Lake, in the land of my fathers. My Paiute name, Thocmetony, means "Shell Flower." I was the fourth child born to my mother, Tuboitonie, and my father, Old Winnemucca. For generations, my people, the Northern Paiutes (or the Numa, as we called ourselves), lived and died on this land. We moved with the seasons, following the food, taking our homes and families with us wherever we went.

My father was an antelope shaman, or charmer. He discovered the location of the antelope herd in his dreams, and then led his people to them.

OPPOSITE: *Sarah Winnemucca, dressed for her speaking engagements in Boston and other East Coast cities. Photo courtesy of the Nevada Historical Society.*

WHERE DO YOU LIVE?

The Northern Paiutes lived in the Great Basin, a desert-area region that gets as little as eight inches of precipitation a year. Because of the dryness of this area, there is little game or vegetation. The Paiutes gathered whatever food they could find, sometimes walking many miles to harvest various crops of roots, grasses, nuts, seed, berries, and reeds. The most common large mammal was the antelope, but the Paiute often had to resort to eating grasshoppers, squirrels, and small rodents.

My mother, like her mother before her, spent her days walking many miles looking for food. In the spring, I helped her gather fresh, soft roots and reeds at the edge of the river. In the summer, we lived and hunted in the coolness of the mountains. And in the fall, we gathered pine nuts and caught enough fish to feed us through the winter. This is the way my people lived. It was a hard life, for this is a harsh land, but it was also a life of abundance, peace, and beauty.

CAPTAIN TRUCKEE: WADSWORTH, NEVADA, AUTUMN 1844

Our white brothers started coming to this land a few years before the birth of Thocmetony, or Sarah, as she is now known. Little by little, in small groups they came. At first they were few and friendly and our people had nothing to fear from them. We all got along, for this is a big land and the Great Spirit provides for all of his children.

Then, in the year of Sarah's birth, I greeted a group of explorers led by Lieutenant John Charles Frémont. I traveled with them east, across the mountains, marveling at the many wonders of the white world. I saw big houses that float on the ocean and travel faster than our horses. I heard the bird's song coming from a huge metal flower hanging in a tower and marveled at the abundance of their winter food supply stacked on shelves in buildings in their villages.

When I came home, I shared all of this with my family. I showed them a letter written by Lieutenant Frémont. I called it my "rag friend." This white paper covered with many black marks talked for me. I used it often, showing it to my white brothers and sisters. After my rag friend talked to them, they trusted me. Sometimes they shook my hand and pounded me on the back with great big smiles shining on their faces. My rag friend became my most prized possession.

SARAH: BEFORE 1850

As time passed, more and more of our white brothers came. Some stayed and camped on our land and some continued on, crossing over the mountains into California. My people greeted all who came with kindness, sharing our precious food with them, for these white men were silly and did not know how or where to look for food.

When winter came, the white people stopped coming. As the snow fell outside, my people sat around the campfire, talking and wondering about these pale-faced strangers. Where did they come from and why? Members from other tribes told us scary stories about these foreigners. We heard that they ate their dead and we learned that they killed Native peoples. Grandfather Truckee talked of the white men's kindness and their wondrous world in California. My father reminded Grandfather how the white men had killed my uncle. I listened to this and my fear of these strangers grew. That winter, whenever I was bad, my

JOHN CHARLES FRÉMONT

Lieutenant John Charles Frémont is sometimes called "The Pathfinder" because he led the first systematic exploration of Nevada for the US Army Topographical Corps. To take him through this uncharted territory, Frémont employed Kit Carson as his guide. He also engaged the help of friendly Native Americans whenever possible. There are some who say that Captain Truckee showed Frémont the way over the Sierra Nevadas into California.

WHAT DID YOU SAY YOUR NAME WAS?

Sarah's grandfather came by his white name, Captain Truckee, through a misunderstanding. When Captain Truckee first met the explorer John Charles Frémont, Truckee stuck out his hand in greeting, saying, "Truckee, truckee." This was the Paiute word for "all right" or "very well." Frémont thought this was an introduction, and from then on called him Captain Truckee. The Truckee River in Nevada is named after Sarah's grandfather.

PINE NUTS

In autumn, the Paiutes gathered to harvest pine nuts from the piñon pine. These nuts were essential winter food. A family of four could gather about twelve hundred pounds of pine nuts, which would last them for about four months. The pinecones were pulled or shaken from the tree and heated in large pits until they opened, releasing the nuts, which were then roasted and ground into meal. When mixed with water, this meal became mush, a staple of their winter diet.

mother told me to behave or a white man would come and eat me up.

Spring came, and with the melting snow and new green grass came a great wave of white people traveling once again through our land. I was glad when my father took us to live in the mountains where we would be safe.

TUBOITONIE, SARAH'S MOTHER: BEFORE 1850

In the fall, we came down from the mountains to fish in the Humboldt River. The women gathered wild seeds and used large round rocks to grind the seeds into flour. We dried fish and berries. When we had enough food, we put it in one place, covered it with grass, and covered the grass with mud until it stuck up from the ground like a wigwam. This is the way we protected our food supplies until winter.

While we worked, we always kept a lookout for the white men. We had heard they had a terrible weapon that sounded like thunder and flashed like lightning, and they used it to kill those that got in their way.

Then one morning we heard that some white people were coming. Frightened, we ran. I put the baby on my back and held Sarah by the hand. But she was too little and couldn't run fast enough to keep up. I feared that we might be killed if we didn't get away. So a friend and I stopped and dug a hole in the ground. We put our little girls inside, covering them up with dirt until only their heads stuck out aboveground. We shaded their faces with sage bushes and warned them over and over again to be quiet. I didn't want to leave Sarah behind, but leaving her was the only way to save her.

SARAH

I cried when my mother left me there all alone. What if the white strangers found me and ate me? The sun crept slowly across the sky while fear pounded in my chest. Minutes passed like hours, and hours passed like days until finally, as darkness fell, my mother and father came and freed me from my dirt grave. We cried and hugged and thanked the Great Spirit for keeping me safe. But that night as I lay beside my parents, I feared the white man even more.

OLD WINNEMUCCA, SARAH'S FATHER

While we hid in the mountains that day, the white people traveled by. They saw the mud cones that held our winter supplies and they burned them. All of our winter food floated away in big clouds of black smoke. We cried when we saw the ashes of our hard work. I looked at my children and thought of the long winter ahead, and my fists tightened and the heat of anger spread across my face.

UP IN SMOKE

Winter was a difficult time for the Paiutes. Ice covered the lakes, snow covered the plants, and most animals hibernated. Therefore, the Paiutes spent eight months of the year gathering enough food to last them for the four winter months. A typical winter meal might have included dried fish and dried vegetables simmered together in a pot to make soup or stew, served with cakes or mush made from pine-nut flour.

CAPTAIN TRUCKEE: SPRING 1850

Wave after wave of white men came into our land. My people had two choices: leave our homeland, or try to live peaceably. Killing the white man wasn't the answer. There were too many of them.

I knew that in order to get along with our white brothers, my people needed to know them, to understand their ways. So I took Tuboitonie and the children with me to California.

SARAH: SPRING 1850

I didn't want to go. I hated Grandfather for making me do this, for taking me away from my home. I said, "No! I won't go!" I stomped my foot and hid my face and when he called to me, I refused to look at him or to sit on his lap.

CAPTAIN TRUCKEE

My little sweetheart, my little Sarah, was filled with fear. But I made her go anyway. She needed to learn about the white man.

So that fall, we took down our camp, loaded our possessions, and made the long, hard journey across the mountains to California. We traveled along the trails already worn deep into the earth by the white men and their traveling houses. It took many days. Some days we traveled and saw no white people. Sometimes our scout came back and told us he saw houses, and sometimes we passed large groups of white people camped along the trail. When this happened, I showed them my rag friend and they gave us flour or bread, or gifts of calico and red shirts.

Sarah

It was on that trip to California that I saw a white man up close for the first time. Grandfather Truckee brought him to our camp. His large blue eyes looked like those of an owl, and his face was covered with hair. I hid under a robe. Peeking out from behind my mother, I quivered and cried as I stared at his ugly face. My grandfather was angry with me. He didn't understand my fear.

When we got to Stockton, California, my people set up camp outside the city. A woman offered us some food, and she looked so kind, and my brothers smiled so big when they tasted it, that I took a piece and put it in my mouth. She called it cake. Its sweetness made me want to eat more and more.

I became very sick. My mother yelled angrily at Grandfather, saying the food of the white woman poisoned me. Grandfather patiently reminded Mother that she let me eat the food without giving thanks to the Great Spirit. But really, it was no one's fault but my own. It was poison oak that made me sick. My face swelled up. I slept fitfully, tossing and turning with chills and fever. My family sat beside me and prayed.

White Townswoman

Captain Truckee came to me, hat in hand, humbly asking me to visit his sick granddaughter. I went with him to the Indian camp. That poor child was so sick and her family so upset that my heart went out to them. Their camp might have been crowded and dirty and their food unappealing, but I realized that they felt the pain of their little girl's sickness the same way I did when my child was sick. After that, I came every day, bringing medicine and nourishing food.

Sarah

At first when the white woman came, I was so sick, and my fevered dreams were so jumbled, that I thought she had come to take me to the Spirit Land. She spoke to me in words I did not understand, and yet the words comforted me. After that, I didn't fear the white people as much. Grandfather Truckee took our family into town to visit his white brothers and sisters.

Tuboitonie: Summer 1850

After Sarah got better, we continued our travels. We stopped at a ranch along the San Joaquin River. The owner knew my grandfather, Captain Truckee, and asked him to take care of his horses. My father said yes, even though I pleaded with him not to leave us here alone with the whites. He smiled and said, "My white brothers won't hurt you. They will teach you how to work and how to speak their language. You will all be friends."

But after he left, the men that Captain Truckee thought were his "brothers" began to come into the camp at night looking for Mary, my oldest daughter. We hid in fear for our safety. Finally, the ranch owner had to let us sleep in the ranch house because he could not control his ranch hands.

Sarah

Once we moved into the ranch house, I liked living with the whites. They had so many beautiful things. I remember the first time I went into the dining room, my heart pounded and my eyes widened. I saw dishes and cups, chairs and a table. I wanted more than anything to sit in the soft red chair. When I asked my mother, she said no, that the white man would whip me if he saw me in it.

Ranch Owner by the San Joaquin River

Some people told me I was a fool to trust the "wild injuns" with my horses and cattle. But the work season ended and those "wild injuns" brought every last one of my animals back to me. I killed several cattle and we feasted together. I paid them with guns and horses. That night they danced joyfully by the campfire to celebrate their good fortune.

There are those who say the Paiutes are savages. But in my experience they are honest and hardworking, gentle and kind.

This photo of an abandoned mine in Nevada shows the harshness of the landscape where the Paiutes lived. Photo courtesy of the Denver Public Library Western History Collection.

THIS IS HARDER THAN IT LOOKS

When white settlers first came to the area, they lumped many of the tribes they saw in northern California and Nevada into one big group. They called them "Diggers." This was a derogatory name that made fun of the fact that they were often seen digging up roots from the ground.

In truth, the Paiutes were expert food gatherers. They knew exactly what food was edible, how it could be used, and where it could be found. Their knowledge gave them the ability to survive in an extremely harsh environment.

SARAH: SPRING 1851

We left the ranch, excited to go home. Traveling many days up and over the mountains, we passed the familiar places of our homeland: beautiful meadows where we dug our roots, large stands of piñon trees where we gathered the piñon nut, the special crook in the river that is the best place to fish. Already we saw a difference. The white man had dug his mines into the mountains, built a city in the meadow, put up sawmills on the crook of the river, and cut down the trees to build their houses. My anger choked me. Why did the white men think it was okay to take our land?

Townswoman: Nevada, Spring 1851

A band of Indians traveled by our house today. A neighbor told me they are called "Diggers" because they dig up most of their food from the ground. They are dirty and will eat anything. Why, I heard they have even been known to eat grasshoppers and rodents! My goodness, they are such savages! They scare me so. When I saw them, I made the children hide in the house while I sat on the porch with the rifle in my lap. You never know what these savages will do. I've heard that they enjoy killing white people for sport. We were lucky. Today they just rode by, looking sadly at our house and the fences we put up around our crops. Why should they be sad? We own this land, bought it from the United States government. We put those fences up to keep wild animals and Indians out!

Captain Truckee

As we came down the east side of the mountains, I smiled in my eagerness to catch the first glimpse of my people, but as they approached I saw their sadness. They carried it on their shoulders wrapped tightly around them like the red wool blankets the white men gave us. Our friends and family greeted us with tears and the terrible news that many of our people who lived along the Humboldt River were dead of a strange illness. When we heard this sad news, we fell into each other's arms, crying.

Sarah

We mourned for our people by cutting our hair, slashing our skin and our clothing, and rubbing our faces and bodies with ashes. In this way, we looked on the outside the way we felt on the inside—cut, bruised, and bleeding.

RITUALS

In her book *Life Among the Paiutes*, Sarah described the rituals they followed after the death of a family member. First, they "cut long gashes in their arms, and they were all bleeding as if they would die with the loss of blood. This continued for several days." She went on to explain that "when the woman's husband dies, she is first to cut off her hair, and then she braids it and puts it across his breast: then his mother and sisters, his father and brothers and all his kinfolk cut their hair. The widow is to remain unmarried until her hair is the same length as before."

Major Ormsby: Genoa, Nevada, 1857

Like many other people in town, we decided to take some Indians into our home. It seemed the Christian thing to do, civilizing those poor heathens.

We lived in Genoa, where I owned a store on the main street. Sarah and Elma came to live with us, worked in the store, and waited on the stage passengers when they stopped here. They also helped my wife with her housework and kept my daughter, Lizzie, company.

Sarah surprised us. She loved to learn. While she lived with us, her language and her reading improved.

Mrs. Ormsby

We treated those two Indian girls very well, indeed. I must say that Lizzie just adored them. Right after they came, we cleaned them up and got rid of their filthy Indian leathers. We gave them clean clothes and sturdy shoes to wear and taught them to fix their hair properly. I must say, they looked so much better, it did my heart good to see them.

Sarah

I don't think that the Ormsbys liked my people very much. They expected me to act like a white girl. I wore white girls' dresses that squeezed my neck and pinched my wrists. I spoke only English, ate only white people's food, and slept in a bed. I was even given a white girl's name—Sarah.

But I liked living with the Ormsbys. There was always plenty of food, and we were never cold or hungry. I missed my family, but there were many other Paiutes living in Genoa, so I didn't feel lonely. While we lived there, everything was peaceful. There was no stealing and everyone got along. Now the whites would know the goodness of the Paiutes. The townspeople trusted us so much that they even gave the Paiute men guns in exchange for their horses. I wanted to ask them why they never gave us anything in exchange for our land, but I didn't.

Everything changed, though, the day two dead white men were brought in—killed by Washo arrows. Three Washo tribe members were brought in to pay for the crime they swore they didn't commit. The three men were thrown in jail. The next day, they got scared when they saw the crowd of angry white men coming to get them. As they ran away, they were shot in

Sarah posing in ceremonial dress. She wore costumes like this for audiences who came to learn more about Native American ways of life. Photo courtesy of the Nevada Historical Society.

THIS ISN'T ANY WAY TO LIVE

The Paiutes soon discovered the truth about the reservation system. They were required to stay on the reservation, and if they were caught outside of it, they were often shot. However, the whites continued to encroach on their land, and soon there weren't enough resources within the confines of the reservation to support the Paiutes. In addition, the food and supplies promised them by the government were never delivered.

the back. I saw their mothers and wives crying over their bodies as they lay bleeding in the street of that friendly town. I saw then that the white men didn't really trust us. To them, we were the enemy.

Later, we learned that the two white men had not been killed by the Washo but by other whites.

OLD WINNEMUCCA: SUMMER 1860

For many years I tried to keep peace with the whites, until one day there seemed to be no solution but war. Two of our little girls were found beaten and tied up at the home of two white men. Our warriors killed the men and burned their house to the ground.

TOWNSPERSON

Those bloodthirsty savages are at it again. This time they have murdered two innocent, hardworking, kind-hearted settlers. We rounded up an army of volunteer soldiers and went on the attack. It is high time we teach those savages a thing or two about justice.

SARAH

War came to my people. It was a very sad time. The men fought while the rest of us hid in the mountains. Major Ormsby, the man I thought was our friend, led the white men into battle against my people. He died, as did many others. Finally the whites said, "No more fighting." We agreed. That is when they offered to put us on a reservation. We saw it as a victory and celebrated with a dance, our hearts light and full of hope, believing that the time of darkness and sadness had passed. Little did we know that it had just begun...

This photograph of the Winnemucca family was probably taken on an 1880 visit to Washington, DC. (Left to right: Sarah Winnemucca, Chief Winnemucca, Natchez, Captain Jim, and an unidentified boy). Photo courtesy of the Nevada Historical Society.

❧ *Afterword* ❧

Sarah and her people were given a stretch of land sixty miles long and fifteen miles wide—just a tiny portion of the place they had once called home. In return for this land, their safety, and regular shipments of food and supplies, the Paiutes promised to keep the peace.

As more and more settlers came into the area, they settled on the Paiute reservation. The government never did send any food or supplies. Sarah's people fell further and further into poverty.

As time passed and Sarah saw the plight of the Paiutes worsen, she looked for ways to help. At first, she and her father put together a stage show and performed in San Francisco and Virginia City. They acted out skits showing their way of life. They raised enough money to feed their family for the winter. After that, with the language skills she had learned from the Ormsbys, Sarah worked for the US Army, translating for her people and making sure that they understood the documents they were being asked to sign.

Conditions continued to worsen for the Paiutes. Sarah thought that if the white people understood their plight they might be willing to help. She wrote letters to the government. She traveled across the United States and Europe, giving more than four hundred speeches. She even went to Washington, DC, where she talked to the Secretary of the Interior and met President Hayes. Sarah was relentless in her attempts to help her fellow Paiutes. People were impressed by her intelligence and touched by her story, but nothing she did seemed to make a difference.

After one of her speeches, she met two sisters from back East. They helped her out with money when she started a school for Paiute children. Her school was very successful, but eventually the US government shut it down, saying that Indians must attend English-speaking boardinghouses.

The two sisters encouraged Sarah to write her autobiography, and when it was done they helped her get it published. Sarah's book was the first book ever written in English by a Native American woman. Published in 1883, *Life Among the Paiutes* is Sarah's biggest success. Through the book, the people of her time learned that this Native American wasn't an ignorant savage. She was articulate, emotional, and intelligent. Thanks to Sarah, readers can learn the story of American expansion through the words and experiences of a Native American woman.

⪥ *Bibliography* ⪥

Ashby, Ruth, and Deborah Gore Ohrn. *Herstory*. New York: Viking, 1995.

Canfield, Gae Whitney. *Sarah Winnemucca of the Northern Paiutes*. Norman: Univ. of Oklahoma Press, 1983.

Dunn, John M. *The Relocation of the North American Indian*. San Diego, CA: Lucent Books, 1995.

Hopkins, Sarah Winnemucca. *Life Among the Paiutes*. Reprint. Reno: Univ. of Nevada Press, 1994.

Parchemin, Richard, ed. *The Life and History of North America's Indian Reservations*. North Dighton, MA: J.G. Press, 1998.

Scordato, Ellen. *Sarah Winnemucca: Northern Paiute Writer and Diplomat*. New York: Chelsea House, 1992.

Seagraves, Anne. *High-Spirited Women of the West*. Hayden, ID: Wesanne Publications, 1992.

Sherrow, Victoria. *Indians of the Plateau and Great Basin*. New York: Facts on File, 1992.

Index

(Note: Page numbers in italics indicate photographs and paintings.)